An Underground Life

LIVING OUT
Gay and Lesbian Autobiographies

Joan Larkin and David Bergman
GENERAL EDITORS

An Underground Life

THE MEMOIRS OF A GAY JEW
IN NAZI BERLIN

Gad Beck

written with Frank Heibert

translated from the German by Allison Brown

The University of Wisconsin Press

The University of Wisconsin Press
2537 Daniels Street
Madison, Wisconsin 53718

3 Henrietta Street
London WC2E 8LU, England

2   4   5   3

Printed in the United States of America

Library of Congress Cataloging-in-Publication Data
Beck, Gad, 1923–
[Und Gad ging zu David. English]
An underground life: memoirs of a gay Jew in Nazi Berlin /
Gad Beck; written with Frank Heibert; translated by Allison Brown.
176 pp.   cm. — (Living out)
ISBN 0-299-16500-0 (cloth: alk. paper)
1. Beck, Gad, 1923–   2. Jews—Germany—Berlin Biography.   3. Jewish
gays—Germany—Berlin Biography.   4. Holocaust, Jewish (1939–1945)—
Germany—Berlin Personal narratives.   5. Berlin (Germany) Biography.
I. Heibert, Frank.   II. Title.   III. Series.
DS135.G5   B333   1999
940.53'18'092—dc21   99-6441
[B]

Special thanks to Wichern Publishers, Berlin,
for the reproduction of the original photographs,
which appear on pages 100–103 and 108.

Partial funding for the publication of this edition was
provided by Inter Nationes, Bonn.

For Miriam, Zwi, and Julius

Search for truth,
Love beauty,
Wish for good,
Do what is best.
　　　　　— *Moses Mendelssohn*

"What is that — optimism?"
"Oh, it is the insanity
to claim that all is well,
even when you are feeling bad."
　　　　　— *Voltaire*, Candide

Foreword

GAD BECK IS A MASTER in the art of living. With just the right combination of daring and ingenuity, humor and design, he faces moments of both happiness and adversity in life, seizes opportunities in both hands, and knows how to draw something positive out of every catastrophe. Doing good deeds and living a good life are not mutually exclusive for him; on the contrary, they are mutually dependent. For only those who savor the pleasures of the senses know how to make sense out of life.

Gad Beck is no preacher. He lived through twentieth-century German Jewish history before it became "world history," and that is why he is able to describe it in detail without the seemingly stilted grief or political correctness often expressed by those wanting to respond "appropriately." He is discerning; he experienced individual people and situations, not "the Germans" or "the Jews." He never loses sight of the overall situation, but it is the details—the small observations and scenes—that will invite readers to empathize, drawing them into the unimaginable time of his childhood and youth, when atrocities were part of everyday experience.

Gad Beck is a fabulous storyteller. His recollections express the fresh, sometimes sunny immediacy of his experience. With his unmistakable mixture of Berlin warm-hearted gruffness, Viennese clever charm, Yiddish chutzpah, and the Oriental art of romancing, Gad Beck builds bridges where others thought the gaps could not be spanned.

FRANK HEIBERT

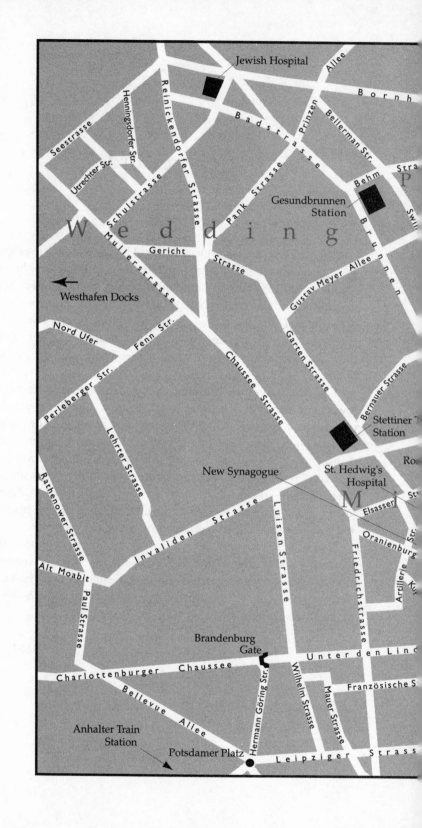

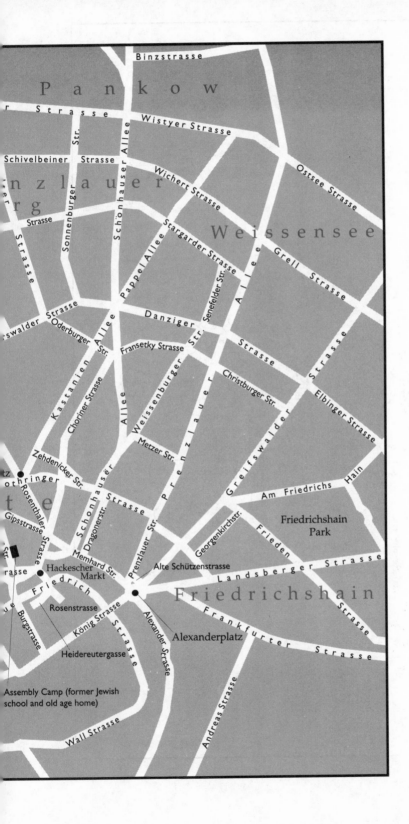

Binzstrasse

P a n k o w

r Strasse

Wistyer Strasse

Schivelbeiner Strasse

Str.

Schönhauser Allee

Ostsee Strasse

Wichert Strasse

n z l a u e r

W e i s s e n s e e

Sonnenburger

Strasse

Stargarder Strasse

Grell Strasse

Strasse

Pappel Allee

Senefelder Str.

Allee

rg

Strasse

swalder Strasse

Oderburger Str.

Danziger

Strasse

Fransetky Strasse

Str.

Christburger Str

Elbinger Strasse

Kastanien Allee

Choriner-Strasse

Allee

Weissenburger

Prenzlauer

Strasse

Metzer Str.

Greifswalder

Zehdenicker Str.

Am Friedrichs Hain

othringer

Schönhauser

Strasse

Friedrichshain
Park

Georgenkirchstr.

Frieden

Gipsstrasse Strasse

Rosenthaler Strasse

Dragonerstr.

Memhard Str.

Prenzlauer Str.

Alte Schützenstrasse

L a n d s b e r g e r   S t r a s s e

Hackescher
Markt

rasse

Friedrich

F r i e d r i c h s h a i n

Rosenstrasse

Burgsstrasse

König Strasse

Strasse

Alexander-Strasse

Alexanderplatz

F r a n k f u r t e r   S t r a s s e

Strasse

Heidereutergasse

Assembly Camp (former Jewish
school and old age home)

Andreas Strasse

Wall Strasse

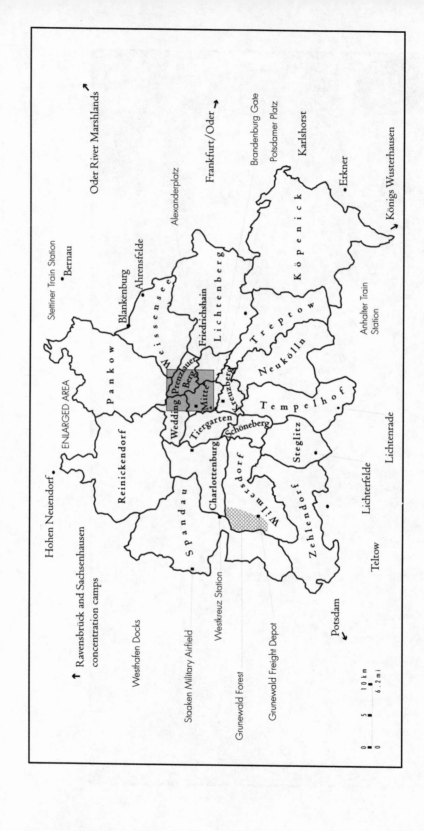

Prologue

S o, that's it!" My life began with these words.
My sister, Margot, was lying on the table kicking her feet and crowing. She was enjoying her new existence. Dr. Neumann wiped the sweat of the stifling late June afternoon from his brow, packed his utensils back into his bag, said goodbye, and was on his way.

And that might have been "it." Might have. My mother was absolutely exhausted, and the midwife was waiting for the afterbirth in order to finish up the job properly. But nothing came. My mother started getting feverish. The midwife knew her stuff. "There's something still in there," she announced dryly and sent the maid off to call back the doctor. He was there in no time, reached inside, and agreed: "Uh-oh! There's another one."

He pulled me out and tossed me onto the table: a boy, but a "blue baby." I didn't let out a sound; things did not look good. Neumann started comforting my father: "You have a wonderful, healthy daughter. . . ."

But the midwife responded with a few well-placed, expert slaps on my little buttocks and managed to get me breathing. I let out a scream. Incidentally, I am absolutely convinced that my zest for life and my optimism can be traced back to this happy last-minute delivery.

My mother too saw the circumstances of my birth as having set the course for my future life. No question about it, my two favorite vices were also born back on that thirtieth of June, 1923. "The only time he was ever blue was at his birth," she commented, her humor really blossoming in the 1950s in Israel, when I was enjoying the good life in the Promised Land, often in quite high spirits. And my mother saw the midwife's heartily slapping life into me as the early sensitization of a body part where my sixth sense would dwell later in life.

3

On the other hand, another early childhood experience had the impact of aversion therapy. As infants, Margot and I would lie next to each other in the twin baby carriage. Now, she was on the outside, her head in the fresh, mild summer breeze, where she could observe the world. But I was the more delicate, sensitive one; as a result, I was sheltered and protected, placed under the much more boring hood of the carriage. That's how we were chauffeured around the Berlin Scheunenviertel, the district of the poorer, Eastern European Jews, where my family lived. Everyone knows that a baby carriage is something especially irresistible for mothers of any age, and the Jewish *mammes* in the Scheunenviertel were no exception. There was one particularly imposing lady, Frau Strasberg, who constantly bent over me with expressions like "Oh, how sw-e-e-e-t!" Each time, two humongous breasts entered my field of vision, darkened the sky, robbed me of my daylight, the air to breathe, the world. No wonder I never enjoyed any sort of desire whatsoever for female breasts.

I never needed more than that to explain why I like boys more than girls. My family didn't either. When you look at it, our lives, especially during my youth, were filled with other problems—real ones. And we came to grips with them, together.

1

O NCE UPON A TIME there were five sisters. I could begin like that, since there was a clear surplus of women in my mother's family. She did have one brother, but he had already set off into the wide world as a young man. He got as far as Thuringia, a good two hundred miles away. In the early twentieth century Hedwig Kretschmar moved with her mother and four sisters from the Oder marshlands to Berlin to look for work. The father had gambled his money away.

Around the turn of the century, absolutely ugly apartment houses were built all over Berlin. Intended to take in the masses attracted to the boom of the capital, they were put up fast and apathetically. The Kretschmars moved into a medium-sized, gray apartment near Gesundbrunnen, in the north of the city. Some of the sisters had to sleep in the hall because there wasn't enough room. The family slaved away in the lower middle class.

In 1913 Hedwig turned eighteen and applied for a job at the Heinrich Beck & Company mail-order firm. Everything imaginable could be ordered wholesale from its catalogue. She worked at the telephone exchange. A switchboard operator was something special in those days, something new, and in a company like that one, it was a really influential position.

It didn't take Hedwig long to start playing the modern woman. She smoked heavily, dressed in the newest fashions, and fell in love with her young boss in no time. Her sisters never managed what she did. They all looked like boring goody-goodies. But she was dazzling—rural freshness refined with big-city elegance. She learned the chic styles from Jewish girl-friends at the company, with their fashionable hats and caps, coats and suits. Thus it was not surprising that Heinrich Beck, nine years her senior, fell victim to her charms.

This liaison was frowned upon in the Protestant Kretschmar household. One sister, Anna, was very religious and didn't have anything at all to do with Jews. The rest of the relatives, who lived in the countryside, were blatantly anti-Semitic. They were constantly pressuring Hedwig: "Why don't you marry Cousin So-and-So? He's a decent Christian." But she didn't listen. She wanted the Jew.

When Heinrich Beck was drafted and fought for Austria-Hungary on the Italian Isonzo front, she sent him letters and packages. He reciprocated with photographs showing him posing proudly with his buddies. A sturdy, mustachioed man he was, with alert eyes and a jovial smile. After the war, from which he returned with several small medals, it was clear to both of them that they wanted to raise a family.

If it had been up to Heinrich Beck, he would have kept the marriage "secular," without any religion. He was part of the upwardly mobile German bourgeoisie—you could call them "liberal conservatives"—and he was not overly religious. But then his family, "the Vienna contingent," put in their two cents' worth.

He did in fact come from Vienna, and although he felt German, he never had German citizenship. His family, originally from Galicia, still spoke Yiddish to each other, and they even wrote it—with Hebrew letters. The family was a typical clan of the Hapsburg empire. The fact that Heinrich "defected" to those Prussians in Berlin after completing business training in Vienna was not cause for much enthusiasm from his father. And now he wanted to marry a *goy?* The case was clear: the new family should have *one* religion, and at the time it was not even up for debate whether he would convert to Christianity.

So Hedwig was a good girl and learned all there was to learn, then converted to Judaism. They married in 1920. They had a *ketubah,* or marriage contract, made, a common practice among Jews. It was authenticated in the highly orthodox Adass Yisrael synagogue, but actually that was only because another, more progressive rabbi happened to be on vacation at the time.

The freshly married couple was evidently not averse to matters of the flesh, since they had two children in the first two years of marriage, one right after the other. Both were sons, which was nothing short of a breakthrough for my mother's family. Finally there were some boys. But both died as infants, the first after only a few weeks—he hadn't even left the Jewish Hospital. The other died after a few months at home on Prenzlauer Strasse, where my parents lived above the family business. The doctors urged them not to try again, since the health risk posed by another pregnancy was too great. But Heinrich Beck would hear nothing of the sort, and soon it was that time again.

In 1923 inflation had just about reached its peak. Still, Heinrich was not in the worst shape financially. He supplied the organizers of large social events with party supplies, favors, and decorations and had excellent connections to people in the fairs and carnivals business. This relative prosperity allowed him to enlist the services of an experienced doctor for his wife, to make sure that nothing went wrong this time. He had known Dr. Neumann for a long time. Neumann later joined the SS, but he remained unwavering in his friendship with us. On the day of the birth, he said to my father: "Dear Heinrich, it would be best if you could give me the money around lunchtime, so my wife can buy some butter with it. It'll be too late if we wait till evening." And so that evening the Neumanns had their butter and my parents had us, Margot and Gerhard.

The whole family was bursting with pride: two such sweet babies—things had gone so well after the two lost children! It was really a shame that the Viennese side of the family had turned their backs on Heinrich. Although my mother had converted to Judaism, they didn't want to have anything to do with Heinrich and his *goyishe mishpokhe*. But my father wouldn't stand for that. One day he pulled himself together, packed his wife and offspring along with the nanny onto the train, and took the whole family off to Vienna.

The Becks' beautiful, spacious apartment was in the predominantly Jewish second district on Obere Donaustrasse. My grandfather was a furrier and earned a good living, thank God, since he had nine children, five of them daughters for whom he would have to supply a dowry.

My father stood facing the heavy door. He lifted the knocker and, after a slight hesitation, let it fall with a bang. A moment later his mother was standing before him. "Heinrich!" she yelled out and flung her arms around his neck. No matter what happens, a mother is always happy when she gets to see her son again. "Come in!"

"No," he responded resolutely, "I can't. I am not here alone. My family is here with me." Hedwig was wearing a white fur coat, especially to impress her furrier father-in-law. She looked like a movie star. Despite the pregnancies, she still had a wonderful figure.

A Jew is by nature a curious being, and old Reuwen Beck was no exception. He was standing back in the hallway, trying to peek around both the corner and his wife to catch a glimpse of his daughter-in-law. The venture was a total success. "Come to me, my children!" he called out as he saw the young woman. From that moment on, he and the whole Vienna family cherished my mother. She was a beautiful daughter-in-law, and on top of that they had twins as grandchildren; that was more than enough to convince them.

They visited us regularly in Berlin, and for their part they impressed the Christian side of the family beyond measure. These elegant, genteel, distinguished Jews from grandiose old Vienna were simply fascinating. It enhanced my father's status tremendously. My Uncle Wolken was the representative for Kodak for all of the Balkans, and he often had business in Berlin. Back then, photography was up and coming, and he later had a large photography business in Vienna until it was no longer allowed. I totally admired this uncle. He was well over six feet tall, wore expensive clothes, and while in Berlin always stayed at the Hotel Fürstenhof near the Anhalter train station. We met him there for coffee and cake or ice cream, just for a few hours, since he never had much more time. But we felt . . . well, that kind of life was my dream. I wanted to be like him someday— not necessarily over six feet tall, but cosmopolitan and self-assured and comfortable living a life of luxury. Staying in a first-class hotel and letting the family come there to meet me—fabulous. In the 1970s I once wrote in a letter to my mother that I was going from one fancy hotel to the next, just like Uncle Wolken. He was still our standard.

My parents kept up an active social life. A friend of my mother's was married to a pastry-cook named Hauke, who put my parents on the guest list for the annual Pastry-Cooks' Ball. In return, my father arranged invitations to the highly elegant Ball of the Austrians. On festive occasions, Heinrich Beck was the life and soul of the party. A sturdy, sandy-haired, good-natured man, he would discreetly but definitely down quite a few and start belting out his Viennese couplets. My mother was always on the alert for the right moment to pump black coffee into him—a diabolical combination at that level of blood alcohol. If things got out of hand, he would excuse himself for fifteen minutes or so, retreat to the men's room, and heave it all up. Then he'd continue happily as though nothing had happened. He felt at ease among the Prussians but could call up his sentimental Vienna soul at any time. After we got our first radio, he often sat in front of it when Viennese songs were played and howled his head off. My father's style of living and cheerful nature were the perfect complement to my mother's Protestant dryness.

Social climbing required the appropriate neighborhood, of course. In 1920, as soon as my parents got married, optimists that they were, they had themselves put on the waiting list for a newly built apartment in

Weissensee, a far better neighborhood. By 1927 our three-and-a-half-room apartment on Buschallee was finally ready for us to move in. It had two balconies and overlooked a garden colony. There were tennis courts and a lake for swimming nearby, and the monthly rent was seventy-one marks.

Our new home became a gathering place for all our Berlin relatives, none of whom lived so well. We met to play cards, eat, drink coffee, listen to the radio, or sit on the balcony. Aunt Trude, my mother's youngest sister, moved nearby with Grandma Wilhelmine Loch (her name, which means "hole," was a great source of laughter for us kids).

Margot and I were terribly spoiled and grew up like two little princesses. She was called Puppe, the little doll, and I was Männe, the little man. This distinction, however, seems more like an assertion than a description if you look at our baby pictures.

Our family took our religious education very seriously, and that meant both our religions. Grandma had gotten used to honoring the traditions and customs of the Jews just as much as her own Christian ones.

Wearing a long, black skirt and a bonnet typical for a widow, the elderly lady walked with us little nippers, one holding her left hand and one her right, to the village church in Weissensee for Christmas, and we all bellowed out, "*Vom Himmel hoch, da komm ich her*"—From heaven on high I come to thee.

At the Passover seder, Grandma made sure that everything was done according to the rituals she had just studied up on. When my father started breaking the matzoh, the unleavened bread we eat at Passover to commemorate the exodus of the Israelites from Egypt (since our ancestors had to leave quickly, before the bread could rise), Grandma interrupted him: "Heinrich, you're supposed to wash your hands first! And where are the bitter herbs?"

Jewish rituals are just filled with concrete symbols, and at Passover the story of slavery and the exodus from Egypt is read aloud each year. Especially for children, it is all very impressive. What does the horseradish, the bitter herbs, symbolize? "The Egyptians made life bitter for the Jewish slaves, forcing them to perform hard work with clay and bricks, and all kinds of work in the fields and other tasks." Grandma knew the story from the Old Testament anyway. In order to welcome "the messenger who heralds the coming of the Messiah," a glass of wine is placed in the middle of the table. Then my mother had to open the door so that Eliahu Hanavi—the prophet and liberator—could come in. Right before that, the glass shook. *He* had taken a sip! We kids were newly inspired every time. Of course, we hadn't noticed that my father had banged the table from underneath.

Grandma Wilhelmine was not the only one in the family who had abandoned her original skepticism toward Jews, trading it in for a serious interest based on our real coexistence. My religious Aunt Anna and her husband, Uncle Paul, represented a kind of original Christianity, which was not all that far removed from Judaism. They too were willing to demonstrate this closeness.

A few years later, in 1936 at my bar mitzvah, something unheard-of happened. A male relative, usually an uncle, has to recite a blessing during the ceremony. No one from Vienna could make the trip—at the time, the Vienna Becks were already having financial troubles—so someone else had to do it. Who volunteered but Uncle Paul, the Christian who loved his Jewish nephew! He let himself be called to read from the Torah, and he stepped to the front. Could he read Hebrew? Not a word. But neither could we. For people like us there was someone to recite the text. Paul had the Torah passage for that week read to him. Of course, he had carefully studied the appropriate section beforehand—it was about Jacob and his sons. When he embraced me, he cried. Many years later he was still very moved when speaking about the event and said it was one of the most significant moments in his religious life. In order to make sure the family was well represented, all of my mother's sisters and their spouses sat in the synagogue—women on one side, men on the other, as is right and proper—and my father was the only Jew! Don't forget that this was 1936. That can truly be seen as a profession of love and acceptance.

My upbringing was marked by this unobtrusive, never explicitly uttered tolerance. Such a devoted, open, and serene form of Christian-Jewish ecumenism, full of good-heartedness, could have forged new directions for Central European culture if Hitler had not destroyed it all.

MY SECOND-OLDEST AUNT was my favorite. Martha. She too was an attractive woman, but in a crude, almost disreputable way. She spoke to everything undignified in me.

Her first marriage was to an actor, Herr Pape. She dreamed of being in the theater herself one day. She traveled with this man, living in a trailer. Back then that was part of being "on tour." Right away he gave her a son, but the baby died not long after its birth. A short time later came a daughter, Inge, who was later to become my favorite cousin. Martha and Pape beat each other. Actually, she beat him—so hard, in fact, that they got divorced before I was even born.

But Martha stayed in the theater. Because her husband had not earned tremendous wages as a traveling actor, she had been forced to learn a job in the trade. She became a prompter and is supposed to have been quite talented. In Berlin she was hired by the Komische Oper, the Comic Opera.

In the late 1920s she moved from her small apartment in the Charlottenburg district to Weissensee. Martha was a fantastic aunt. Her life was pretty
adventurous for the times. She had a number of lovers—actors, of course;
she wore extravagant clothing and rings that mysterious men had given her.

Martha spoiled us twins with children's costumes she got from the
opera. Once I was Napoleon! And she gave us cloth to play with, silk and
silver brocade that we would drape around ourselves. I made the most delightful skirts and dresses and developed the theatrical airs and graces of a
diva. It was the only time in my life that something like that was so much
fun for me. I am convinced that my sister learned it all from me: crossing
my legs, laying my hand on the low-cut neckline of my dress, making eyes,
throwing back my head. . . .

My parents were not particularly impressed, especially when I ran
around in my fantasy robes for days. "Son, you just aren't supposed to run
around like that," my father once said. And my fresh response: "But you
loved it when Mommy wore this type of thing!" There was never any pressure or preaching, though, and I was never very shy.

When I was six, in the winter of 1929, thanks to wonderful Aunt
Martha I got a tiny role at the Comic Opera. My debut was in *Die goldene
Meisterin* (The Golden Master Craftswoman), and I even got to sing an
especially sophisticated little song: "Please give me a little dolly, whose
eyes do peekaboo; the sweetest little dolly, who's charming just like you." It
later became a hit. I also performed in *Peterchens Mondfahrt* (Little Peter's
Trip to the Moon) and, well, that was it. A born star.

It was my first encounter with the arts, and it really got everyone
going: "The boy has to learn something artistic." I was given a violin,
and a violinist came to our home twice a week; my aunt paid for my lessons. This teacher was very clever. He always accompanied me so that it
sounded really good to my mother listening in the kitchen. "The boy is
really making progress!" No chance! I was the most untalented violinist
that the world has ever heard. Once I performed a solo at a family gathering. It was a traditional folk song, "Grandma, Grandma," and the audience
almost peed in their pants from laughing so hard. My competition was
Cousin Gerda. She was almost worse than me. When she finished playing
"Ave Maria" there was an awkward silence. The tension was finally broken when she asked how everyone liked it and they all broke out laughing.
No one even had the slightest notion what she had played.

Things started going downhill financially for my father in 1930. He simply
was not a very clever businessman. When the company went into a spin
and he had to give it up, for some reason his partner ended up in a much

better position than he did. At least he was able to continue the mail-order business on a smaller, independent scale. He took a lot of customers with him and ran it all under my mother's name. That involved updating the catalogue each year on his own and sending it out. When orders came in, he would pick up the merchandise from the manufacturers and ship the orders directly to the customers. That might sound unbelievably labor-intensive, and it was. My father almost worked himself to death.

It was not enough for us to live on. His regular orders were also far too uncertain. So he organized another source of income with the help of some Jewish friends. It was a wholesale business in tobacco, cigars, and cigarettes that he operated from our apartment. He had to build up a clientele of tobacco shops and kiosks. He would pick up the merchandise in the morning and deliver it in the afternoons. In the winter he used a sled. Margot and I helped him sometimes. We would take the bus that stopped right in front of our house and deliver the packages.

One customer had a cigarette kiosk at the end of the bus line in Ahrensfelde, east of Berlin. His name was Herr Erich Möller, and he would later become the notorious Gestapo Möller. Every time Margot and I went there, either he or his wife would give us a lollipop and some kisses and send us on our way. I never could have imagined the circumstances under which I would meet Möller again fifteen years later.

Margot and I started school in Weissensee in 1929, when we were six years old. The cutoff date was the end of June, so we were the youngest and smallest. Except for a few recently built streets, Weissensee was still very much like a village; in the summer the fields sprayed with manure around the corner stank to high heaven. Our elementary school was just as countrified.

There were two Gypsies in my class who became good friends of mine. They lived fifteen minutes from our home in Berlin's largest Gypsy tent and caravan camp. The two Herzbergs had been left back a couple of times and were correspondingly older and stronger than I was. They did not attend school with much regularity; sometimes they traveled around with their family and didn't even live in Berlin.

My two "big friends" protected me, and I admired them. With them, I developed my first feelings of devotion and a need to snuggle up, since I saw them as the very epitome of masculinity. They were extremely physical with each other, which was new for me. They touched each other a lot, clumsily and lovingly with rough, knobby hands.

I had another friend in my class, Klaus Schulze. His father was a secondary school teacher in math and biology. We visited each other in the afternoons, on birthdays, for picnics. On one of those visits, the father advised my parents: "Why don't you let Gerhard skip a year? I am sending my son to the *gymnasium* already, and his grades are good enough!" And so at nine years old I started at a *gymnasium,* a prestigious, college-track secondary school.

My parents were pleased but rather surprised. They could definitely not be considered intellectuals. They had brought a tremendous library, all of three books, to their marriage and displayed them in a glass case between chocolate bars, knickknacks, and other ornaments. The books were *Faust, a Tragedy — Part One,* which my mother was given when she finished school, *The Frog with the Mask* by Edgar Wallace, and finally *Der Bürger* (The Bourgeois) by Leonhard Frank, a left-wing book. Someone must have palmed it off on my parents at some time. That was it. By now, my sister and I had collected some books of our own: *Nesthäkchen* (The Baby of the Family) by Else Ury, a Jewish author who was later killed in Auschwitz, *Quo Vadis,* and such. I was already a bookworm as a child.

Whenever I felt sad or depressed about something I withdrew. I'd lie down quietly in my bed and cuddle with my dolls until I felt better. I really did have dolls, especially one boy doll! When I was eight or nine my parents gave me a typically Bavarian-looking Seppl doll — strange educational methods. Margot was insulted. She had all these stupid dolls with porcelain heads, babies with crooked legs, goggly eyes, and red cheeks, and then I get this magnificent guy! He had long, powerful legs, a handsome face, and a smart-looking Bavarian hat. I guess he was my first love.

Margot was jealous. No wonder! There we'd be, lying in our beds, and I'd be acting out scenes — "So, now I have Seppl in the car and, bang, I slam the door shut!" Then I would put my arms around him, hold up the pillow to block her view, and cuddle with him. She lay there all alone with her dumb, bowlegged baby dolls. For sure she would have loved to have this "man" in bed. Of course, she couldn't tell any of that to our parents. And I was selfish enough to parade my "lucky love" brazenly in front of her.

It did not take long for Seppl to be replaced by a flesh-and-blood candidate — not in my bed, of course, but in the elaborate fantasies I unfolded in front of Margot. It happened like this. In 1932 we joined a German-Jewish youth group. It's important to emphasize what kind it was since at the time there were a number of different youth groups, ranging from the nationalist Free Youth Movement to Zionist groups. All of them resembled the Boy and Girl Scouts to some extent, lots of sports and field trips and so on. Our first group was a real example of German-Jewish assimilation. These were the first groups to be put under pressure, as the mixing of "Aryan" and

Jewish was a particular thorn in the side of the Nazis. Until the German-Jewish Youth Ring was forced to disband in 1935, Margot and I remained members along with four girls from the neighborhood.

Of course I had a big crush on one of the boys there. He didn't know anything about it, but I concocted the most elaborate romantic adventure fantasies. Again, poor Margot had to listen to all of it. *He* was attacked by the other boys and had to run away. Since he didn't know where to go, he came to me for protection. I took care of him and comforted him. He slept in my bed with me. We were bosom buddies and stuck together.

One evening Margot had had enough of it and started crying. "What's the matter?" I asked, totally surprised. "Can't he sleep with me for once?" Poor thing! I was always making her life difficult, yet she always remained loyal.

Besides my father, Uncle Paul was the most important male adult of my childhood. Paul Krüger lived and worked in the district of Wedding, a pretty rundown area back then. An electrician, he was part of the economic boom brought on by technological progress; in fact, he was responsible for bringing electricity to the apartments that were changing over from gas, and he was very busy. Sometimes, if the people couldn't pay for the modernization, he did the work for nothing. Uncle Paul was a good man.

The Krügers had had a small son whom Paul absolutely adored, but he died when he was five. Then they had a girl, my cousin Gerda, whom Paul didn't like at all. His longing was clearly directed toward a son.

This family was hard for him—girls were skipping around all over, skirts and frills everywhere. But then there was me! This was one more reason for Uncle Paul to come visit us a lot. He really grew fond of me, and I thought he was wonderful. He gave the impression of having a simple disposition, but that wasn't the case at all. He was shy and reserved, and in truth he really needed tenderness. His wife, Anna, was prudish in a Protestant way, and his own daughter didn't mean all that much to him. But on his visits with us he was a warm-hearted uncle who gave us playful pats, strokes, and cuddles. Of course he couldn't snuggle with me and ignore Margot, so she benefited as well. But I was the only one who got to sit on his lap.

When the whole family would sit on the balcony, he would often say, "Annie"—he always addressed his wife, even when he meant someone else —"I have to write a few bills." He'd say it, take his things, and withdraw to the children's room. There he would sit at the big table, and he really would write bills. He only had time to do it on Sundays. All of his work hours were written in a big book, and he would transfer them to invoice forms.

And then it happened for the first time. I must have been about nine years old, and he was in his mid-fifties. I went into the children's room too. Maybe I wanted to get something, I don't remember. As I walked in, he put his pen down immediately and looked at me. I entered and threw a curious glance toward the bills on the table. He put me on his lap and kissed me on both cheeks. It tickled so, because he had a big Kaiser Wilhelm mustache. And suddenly I felt that I was sitting on something! It was warm and firm and felt . . . well . . . nice. He put his arms around me and squeezed me. I cherished every second. Nothing else happened. Not until later did I pay any attention to what was happening in his pants. But he never tried to go any further. He liked it, I liked it. There was an unspoken agreement between us, and we never talked about it. Why should we? He smiled at me in a special way, mischievous and at the same time loving, which is why I tried to provoke these situations.

Such touching was new for me. For the first time, I had erotic feelings in that bottom of mine that had been slapped to get some life into me. The fact that it didn't leave him cold either only served to encourage me. And so we both experienced the fulfillment of our secret desires.

2

"EVERYONE ASSEMBLE IN THE COURTYARD and line up in rows," came the announcement one day in my school before class started. Together with my classmates, I did what I was told; fifteen ten- to twelve-year-old fifth-graders in shorts marched down the stairs. Joined by all the other grades, we streamed into the schoolyard with a military-sounding clatter.

The Nazis introduced a practice to all schools: At the *fahnenappell* every morning before classes started, we all had to gather in the courtyard; the swastika flag was raised, and on command the entire school saluted. On this spring day in 1933, the drill took place for the first time.

All of a sudden, my teacher raced over to me, pointed his index finger in my direction, and ordered in a raspy voice: "Beck, step forward!" I didn't understand. "Step out of line, Beck! We don't mean you! You're a Jew!"

I had to stand in a corner of the schoolyard opposite everyone else. I was the only Jew in my class; there were a few other lost souls from other classes milling around near me. Then came the command, and with a loud bang all the heels snapped together and hundreds of boys' arms shot into a Nazi salute, pointing at us like bayonets. Every morning the spectacle was repeated. We no longer belonged; we were outcasts who were not worthy of saluting the German flag.

Of course, at first we children didn't feel the changes in the political atmosphere as much as the adults did. Whatever had been in the offing before 1933, we were unaffected by it, perhaps shielded from it. But once the German people elected Hitler, things intensified everywhere. You had to be blind and deaf not to notice. Signs telling people to "Boycott Jews!" appeared everywhere; the most sheltered of children could not miss them.

16

My father started feeling the effects in his business relations, but he never spoke to us about it. By then, however, my own experiences sufficed.

Up to that time I had been one of the well-liked pupils. I was always in a good mood, lively and funny. Then all of a sudden strange things started happening. "Herr Teacher, can I sit somewhere else? Gerhard stinks like sweaty Jewish feet!" Children are more direct and brutal than adults. That kind of rejection really hurt. I was ten years old. I didn't understand. But I was not about to accept it as some new standard.

On the day of that first *fahnenappell* I ran home from school crying. It took a while for my helplessness to turn into rage. At lunch I told my family what had happened. My parents' reaction disappointed and confused me totally. They evidently didn't take the event seriously! Soothingly, they babbled on about how things would calm down, how it was just in the beginning that the Nazis wanted to demonstrate that the times have changed, and so on and so forth.

What was that supposed to mean? The Nazi flag was raised and saluted every day, and every day I experienced that old friends no longer wanted to talk to me or play with me, and all because they were "Aryan," something that no one had wasted a thought on before. In the neighborhood, when we were outside playing, the children started separating into "Aryan" and Jewish groups. My parents smiled and tried to placate me. Since Margot had a lot of Jewish friends at her school, she didn't go through the same experiences I did, and so I was alone with my problem.

Actually, it was not all that surprising. My parents were politically in the moderate center, as part of the conservative middle class. They instinctively did everything they could to keep from getting involved in the political turmoil of the times. Their attitude toward Zionism was also typical. My father dismissed the pioneers in Palestine as poor fools who for some obscure reason slogged away in the swamps of Tel Aviv. "What do they want there? We are Europeans; for us it's out of the question anyway."

There was a Jewish family in the apartment building next door. Herr and Frau Cohen were both active Communists. One day in the summer of 1933 we saw a large SA squad marching to the athletic field near Buschallee, our street. On the way, a group of men pushed their way into the Cohens' apartment and beat them up. It was the first time I had ever seen such a display of violence and power. My father seemed concerned, but for him it was not the SA attacking a Jewish family. After he had gotten over his initial shock, he said, "Well, anyone so openly Communist as he is has to reckon with something like that."

He didn't want to believe that the tide had turned and that the Jews—

we!—were also a thorn in the side of the Nazis. *We* had not done anything wrong! If you didn't cause any trouble, you wouldn't suffer any consequences. That's what he believed. In this respect, as well, my father was not all that different from many "Aryan" citizens who did not want to see what was brewing in the upper echelons.

I still had three friends at school. My best friend was a black-haired Romanian boy, two years older than me and of course much bigger. We sometimes played an early pubescent variation of doctor. After school he took me to the school basement and pulled me lovingly to him, rubbing himself against me and arousing himself. It all went into his pants, and then he ran home soaked; it didn't seem to bother him at all. I needed this closeness and affection, even though I didn't really understand all of what was happening. Another friend was a slightly disabled boy who always accompanied me on my way home. The third was from Alsace. He had grown up in a French environment and felt like a stranger in Berlin. In a word, we were all outsiders. Klaus Schulze, my buddy from elementary school, was in a different class, and we lost touch. I felt alone. Nothing really motivated me, and of course my grades suffered.

I started pressuring my parents more and more to take me out of that school. But they didn't want to hear anything of it. They were actually really happy that I was considered gifted and was receiving a promising education at a *gymnasium*. So as things went, I was forced to have more and more to do with the few older Jewish students. They told me there was a "Jewish school," also a *gymnasium*, on Grosse Hamburger Strasse.

Now I would have a counterargument for my parents when they started with their continuing education thing. My father was appalled. Is that why he abandoned the Yiddish of his family and became a good Prussian? So his son could run to the "Jewish school"? No way.

I tried every trick I could think of to convince my parents that the situation was serious. Once I broke my violin bow and complained that bullies had done it. Another time I jumped fully clothed into the pond in front of Margot's middle school in Weissensee and said I was pushed in. I needed a witness. Soaking wet, I slogged out of the water, and Margot got terribly worked up. "They threw my brother in the lake! They can't do that." She made a big commotion, complaining to her teachers. I was dried off and sent home. But my mother was not easy to convince, and she made sure no one bothered my father much with complaints.

In early 1933 Heinrich Beck had already consulted with Uncle Wolken about whether it might not be better, in view of the Nazi government, if our family moved back to Vienna. But with great foresight they came to the conclusion that the Christian side of the family could protect my father and help him through these times. What could they have known back then about what was to come! My smart uncle also thought that things would be more under control with the Prussians than in Austria, where, again and again, anti-Semitism flared up and was allowed to romp uncontrolled.

So for the summer of 1933 my parents did not plan a trip to Vienna, which might have been expected, but instead put Margot and me on a train to Friedrichsroda, a small resort town in Thuringia, to visit with the family of my mother's brother. It was my last carefree summer vacation outside of Berlin. Heinrich and Hedwig had spent their honeymoon there, and Uncle Wilhelm and Aunt Dora were just about in love with my father. Wilhelm was a fat, harmless drinker, and my aunt was indescribably ugly and skinny. She weighed only a little over eighty pounds, but she was just as sweet and kind as her husband. In my first letter home, I wrote—literally— "Aunt Dora is the ugliest woman I have ever seen, but also the nicest!"

After that, the only trips we took were with our classes. We often went away for a week at a time. In the spring of 1934 we went to Bad Schandau, in the idyllically beautiful "Switzerland of Saxony," a hilly part of Saxony near the Czech border. One afternoon we took a hiking trip over the border into Czechoslovakia. Back then brown suede jackets were in fashion, and nine of the fifteen boys in our group had one. They weren't allowed into the country because brown was the Nazi color! My mother had made me a jacket just like that in gray. My teacher thought for a minute and then decided to go over with the remaining six of us for an hour or two. The others had to wait until we returned. That was the first time I experienced a kind of privilege because I did *not* belong to the Brownshirts!

A short time later I had appendicitis and had to go to the hospital. When I came home, our apartment had been transformed into a sickroom. Aunt Frieda had moved in with her critically ill husband.

In the 1920s she had married Heinrich Uhde, a bank director from Magdeburg. He was quite a find; they lived in a luxurious villa in Bad Salzelmen, not far from the city. He was a loving, softhearted man with a handsome face, but he had no neck, and his large head was propped on a body that was so hunchbacked he could hardly walk. Now all the health problems that come with such a hump had worsened to such an extent that my uncle could barely stand it. The constant painkilling injections had turned him into a morphine addict. His private bank had to be liquidated. He could no longer manage it and spent far too much money.

"Uncle Heine" was always patient and kind to us kids, despite his agony. Maybe that's why I never sensed any repugnance at the sight of hunchbacks. Very early on I noticed how sensitive and needy they are, since most people reject them. Later I often encountered hunchbacked or crippled men, sometimes in sexual situations, but I never felt any reluctance.

Right after the Uhdes moved in with us, it became clear that our uncle was dying. We were all terribly upset, yet we didn't really want to shout from the rooftops that he was addicted to morphine. My parents called Dr. Neumann, who had meanwhile become a total Nazi. He came to examine the patient and of course caught on immediately to what the situation was. There were even hypodermic needles and ampoules lying all around the bed.

Neumann threw my parents a sinister glance and scolded: "Are you crazy? Taking in a morphine addict? Get the man out of here as fast as possible! You're a Jewish household! Don't you know what kind of trouble you could get into?!"

He arranged for an ambulance. My uncle couldn't even lie down; he had to be transported sitting. By the time they got him to the hospital he was dead. DOA. Neumann signed the death certificate and thus helped us out of a jam—regardless of what kind of Nazi he was.

Then something happened at the school sports festival in the summer of 1934. I was the final runner in the four-man sixty-meter relay.

The teacher stood at the finish line, and I was the first to run past him. My team had won! There was great excitement. I was proud as anything, and so was my mother, sitting in the stands with Aunt Trude. But my teacher pulled me aside and whispered, "You know you can't stand with the others on the victory platform!" He looked somewhat helpless and regretful, but his hands were tied. According to his regulations I was really not allowed to be honored since I was Jewish. My world collapsed at that moment. I was the first to cross the finish line and wasn't allowed to stand up there with the rest. . . . The teacher turned and went over to the other three. Then he looked for a fourth who could stand on the podium in my place.

My mother observed the situation and froze. She finally understood. The next day she stormed into the principal's office: "I will not allow you to shatter my child!" The school principal was a reasonable man. "Frau Beck, we don't have much leeway. You know, I am sending my own children to the French high school. It's the only school in Berlin where the instruction is still neutral and unprejudiced. Look around for another school where you can register your children. That's my sincere advice."

The man was soon replaced by a Nazi. After I had fought for a whole year, my mother finally conceded and sent me to the Jewish School on Grosse Hamburger Strasse. That marked my return to the Scheunenviertel.

Until then my education and development had been influenced more by Christianity than by Judaism. Our Jewishness had been limited to celebrating the holidays and to our religious instruction, which Margot and I attended a few afternoons a week, like going on a pilgrimage from our nondenominational school. Actually, I liked those classes a lot, even if my religious feelings were very limited.

At the Jewish School for Boys and Girls I immediately felt better. All that I had experienced had led me in the only direction still open to me, the Jewish one. My sister's transition did not progress as quickly. She had felt neither the pressure of the Nazis nor the temptation of escaping into a Jewish environment as strongly or as early as I had. My mother suffered terribly at the loss of the Christian-Jewish world that we had built up together. I was the first in my family who made it clear to all of us: The Jewish way was the only way left for us, and that's the way I was going.

All the depression I had been packing away in myself in the last year at the school in Weissensee disappeared. No, it was more than that. My desire to learn grew much stronger, to grow into a community that was mine, that I fit into, and one that did not question my integration in the slightest. At this point at the latest it became apparent that I was not a loner or individualist who thrives on making it in a hostile environment. Groups and community were always important to me, where I could do something, organize something, and earn recognition.

The curriculum at the Jewish School was the absolute opposite of that at my old school. It carried a clear, albeit unspoken, mission of giving the students useful tools for emigration. Thus we learned foreign languages: Hebrew, English, French, and afternoons, as an elective, Spanish. I really enjoyed languages a lot. German was also important, of course. Biology, chemistry, and physics, on the other hand, were not given much emphasis. As a result, everything I couldn't stand was omitted anyway—dissecting frogs on a lead plate and stuff like that. Suddenly my grades improved.

Then there was, of course, sports! I wasn't bad, but for me the main thing was the eroticism of athletics. In one exercise, all the boys would stand in a line, one behind the other. The last in the line had to hold a ball and crawl through the legs of the other boys all the way to the front, and then the next would go. What a spectacular view! Or we'd have to climb up a pole and then slide down. Half the boys had wet gym shorts from the rubbing. I enjoyed that the way some people nowadays enjoy porno films.

My first real sexual experience happened during physical education—with my gym teacher. I was twelve; he was twenty-two. Since, as a Jew, he was prohibited from continuing his studies at the university, he was hired as a teacher's assistant. After official school hours, he worked out with individual students on a voluntary basis. I was still running the relay, but he wanted to win me over to jumping hurdles—actually a silly idea considering my short legs.

One day I was his last student. When practice was over, we went to the showers. He was in one corner, and shyly I went to the other end of the shower room. He finished before me, put on a bathrobe, and threw me a towel. In that moment I was overcome with unrestrained desire. Without thinking about what I was doing, I went over to him and snuggled into his bathrobe, naked. Not a word was uttered. Thank goodness! I would not have known what to say. I felt like doing it and I did—it was enough just dealing with that.

I embraced him and noticed that he was aroused as well; I relished the feeling. We caressed and rubbed against each other, not even all that much, and then we came, both of us. The nicest thing for me was that he reciprocated the affection by putting his arms around my shoulders. I had taken him by surprise, but when it happened, he wanted it too, there was no doubt about it.

I ran home beaming with delight. "So, how was your day at school today?" my mother asked as she did every day, throwing me a scrutinizing look. I was incredibly and obviously happy. "Really nice," I reported breathlessly. "After practice I hugged my gym teacher in the locker room. It was really fun." As unbelievable as that might sound, that is how naive I was.

If something had happened with a girl in my class, I probably would have been afraid to say anything. We did at least know that much about this serious thing reserved for grown-ups, which had something to do with having children. But being affectionate with a male teacher? What could happen? Certainly I couldn't get pregnant.

My mother's reaction was just as baffling—she was not at all upset. "Aha, I thought so," she answered dryly. She knew her son was delicate and rather feminine. I never fought with the other boys; instead, I often competed with my sister to see who was more ladylike. Besides, my mother remembered the Seppl doll she had given me; she evidently saw my development as rather consistent.

I came out, as you say nowadays, in a totally nonchalant fashion; it just happened. I never had any feeling that it was wrong to accost my teacher in the shower. It happened spontaneously, just like when my dog wants a sock to chew on and simply jumps up and grabs it.

I never talked about it openly with my parents, but it wasn't necessary. They knew, and later, when I was an adult in Israel, there were certainly times they offered their opinions on concrete situations in my often complex love relationships.

With my gym teacher, by the way, things never went beyond that one experience. I knew very well that I could not catch him unaware again. A few weeks later I was with him alone in the locker room again and went over and hugged him, like the first time. Of course, this time we were both dressed. He was wearing sweat pants, which by no means concealed his physical reaction. But he did not let it go any further this time. He surely was also afraid of the possible consequences. He hugged me very gently and pushed me aside. That made things crystal clear.

But that wasn't really so bad. He had done something for me. And I have never forgotten the happiness of that first encounter. That teacher is now living in Holland. He's over eighty, has been married for an eternity, and has a number of grandchildren. He probably wouldn't even remember who I am.

My first real relationship was with a picture-perfect boy named Otto. He was from Prague. His mother had died, and he lived with his father near the Weissensee station. We would have sex after doing sports or going swimming, and soon I started visiting him at home. Sometimes we could even have our fun there, since his father worked during the day. We finished school around lunchtime, and I would go home with him; then, an hour later, I would be sitting on the streetcar on my way home.

Otto was not the only one. Very soon I started feeling a curiosity toward all kinds of people. It was not purely sexual but mixed with friendly, social, happy feelings. How far I went varied considerably. Except for one man, who was older than I was and very masculine, and who was almost rough with me, I would describe my friends during my youth and the experiences we shared as primarily affectionate and playful. That's what was important to me. The encounters did not have anything to do with love, or even being "in love." That came later.

Another playmate of mine was Martin, who now lives in Vienna as a writer. Back then he lived in the Jewish orphanage. Despite his young fifteen years, Martin smoked very heavily. I used to steal cigarettes from my father for him; that's why he liked me so much. He was a mischief-maker but highly intelligent, which made him an absolute horror for the teachers. I was especially attracted to his impudence.

Martin's speciality was fooling around in broad daylight on the S-Bahn, the elevated suburban railroad. The train was crowded; we would stand really close together and touch each other, rubbing a bit, fumbling around and grabbing. No one around us would notice, or care to notice. We extended our little game to English class, where we sat next to each other. We would jerk each other off under the desk, and our teacher, Fräulein Goldstein, had no idea what was going on. During this phase I felt perfectly content in school.

T HE FAMILY'S FINANCIAL PROBLEMS took a major turn for the worse in 1935. My father, who was going on fifty, was still slaving away with his wholesale tobacco business so his two children could go to the college-track secondary school. Since we were Austrian citizens, our school tuition was higher than the Germans'. At first he still sold merchandise he could get through his connections to the mail-order trade at the Christmas market. But on top of everything, Jews lost their concession permits for outdoor markets beginning in that year.

By this time our Christian relatives had already started helping us out financially. It was all handled very lovingly, very unassumingly. When we went shopping at the outdoor market together, for instance, one of my aunts would pay for everything, explaining, "We'll be getting together at your place again on the weekend anyway."

In exchange, my father got them all the most wonderful things at wholesale prices. As long as he could, he gave fabulous presents for birthdays and Christmas. In any case, we kids never had the feeling of being supported by the rest of the extended family.

Since I was happy at my new school, I was virtually unaware of how the political climate was becoming increasingly distressing and oppressive. When I happily and casually talked about what I was doing, the thing my mother and my aunts heard was that suddenly everything was Jewish. It was alienating for them, especially since things had always been so different. Aunt Trude once broke down in tears, crying: "Why do you always have to isolate yourselves like that? As if the only people who exist for you anymore are Jews!" As naive as that was, it expressed the pain she felt that a rift seemed to be forming between the two sides of our family.

Since we had less and less leeway for development, the decision to focus on my Jewish identity and later Zionism introduced me to something that opened new prospects for the future. The goal was Palestine, homeland of the Jews.

I got involved in more and more activities, which pushed my family into the background. For instance, Sunday had always been the day the entire extended family met at our place. Now I would go on outings or to the Jewish stadium with my group, or we'd go swimming in Lake Oranke. When we would set off to go swimming as a group, my mother would stand on the balcony and shake her head. "Look, Heinrich, there are so many of them, and they all look so Jewish!"

If in the early and mid-1930s there was any Jewish pride in Germany, except for a few isolated Zionists, then it became visible—paradoxically—in competition with the "Aryans." That is the only way to understand the unbelievable article responding to the boycott of Jewish shops that the Nazis had launched on April 1, 1933. In the April 4 edition of the *Jüdische Rundschau*, a Zionist newspaper, the following appeared: "Wear it with pride—the yellow star!" It was a horrendous premonition of the compulsory wearing of the Star of David, a well-meaning and serious reaction to the debasement by the Nazis. There was an incentive to prove, especially now, that Jews were worthy as well—everywhere that "Aryans" were supposedly superior.

In my awakening political identity, I never posed the question of a comparison. I had no desire to try to receive acknowledgment in places where I was not wanted. It seemed pointless and uninteresting.

I also quickly realized that there were limits to the support offered by my Christian relatives. They stood by us; their political attitudes were certainly affected by their having Jewish relations—no one from the generation of my aunts and uncles was a member of the Nazi Party—but of course they were also not in a position to change our situation significantly.

One day a man with serious intentions appeared in the life of my exciting Aunt Martha: Alfred Ludwig, an engineer and bridge-builder. They spent their summer vacation together at Arendssee. The other aunts were already gossiping enviously. Unfortunately, the engineer was already married and lived in Berlin's Lichtenberg district with his wife and daughter.

His wife had been a lady-in-waiting at the court of the last German emperor when she was younger. Now she was seriously ill, dying of cancer. One day she called my Aunt Martha to her and declared her to be her successor. "Take good care of my husband and my child!" Martha cared for the woman until she died.

Alfred Ludwig—whom everyone just called Wobbi—and Martha did not wait long before marrying. That was the first big wedding I attended. The aunts were all standing in front of the church lavishly dressed. The bride wore a black chiffon dress with a slit up the side (a wedding in white was unthinkable for a divorcée), and the celebration was at the café in the park of the Weissensee palace.

Uncle Wobbi came from a left-wing family and thus had nothing to do with the Nazis. He showed an immediate liking for my father. He thought the small Jewish man was delightful. So they often came to visit, driving up in their Opel with their two daughters from previous marriages, Martha's hunchbacked Inge and Wobbi's Ingelies. We went on outings with them together in the car, which was still something special back then. After her years of moving around, Martha now developed her settled side. The Ludwigs set up their new domicile in Lichterfelde-Süd, in the south of Berlin — Martha's apartment was too small, and Wobbi's had too many old memories — and they planned to build a villa in Teltow.

Aunt Frieda, on the other hand, after losing her husband and her villa in the country, had to become somewhat more worldly, for better or worse. She helped out Uncle Paul and lived there during the week. Weekends she spent with us. She gradually became a loud and unbearable nag. One day the woman who owned the newspaper stand on Buschallee told my father about one of her regular customers: "A very charming man. A tailor, very much in demand, all kinds of celebrities and barons and counts go to him. And on top of that, he is very sweet! But he is desperately searching for a wife. . . ."

Telesfor Pannewitz was born out of wedlock to a member of the Polish nobility who had acquired German citizenship. He really did know his trade well. After the war, even Marshal Zhukov, who liberated Berlin with the Red Army, had a suit made by Telesfor.

My father's ears pricked up, and my parents met the man. He was, as befitted his status, incredibly elegant and lived in a beautiful apartment not far from us. Over coffee, he told my parents how well he managed his life. "I take care of everything myself, but I feel so lonely. I need someone in my life!" Finally my father dared to put in: "Would you like to meet my sister-in-law?"

Frieda came to our place on the weekend, and my father said to her in his most charming, lighthearted Viennese chutzpah style, "Gee, you'll never guess who I met. A former comrade from my soldier days!" Well, he was of Polish descent; it *could* have been the truth. He was full of praise for Telesfor, and Frieda smelled a rat. She was furious. "What are you thinking of!? No way will I come here next weekend!" She didn't want to remarry! But somehow my parents managed to get the two of them together. Telesfor came to visit; Frieda was sitting at the coffee table shaking like a leaf. "I thought she would pass out any minute and fall onto the cake," my mother later told me.

The matchmaking efforts were at least halfway successful. Telesfor found Frieda absolutely enchanting and put on all the moves of a gentleman in search of a bride. He was generous, gallant, witty, patient, cheerful . . . everything a woman could want. He was evidently thus able to arouse feelings in her; maybe she couldn't resist the security, the protection. In any case, they got married in 1936. We organized the wedding in our big apartment; it was a fabulous party. We still had our fancy clothes from Martha's wedding the year before, and we celebrated as joyously as we could.

Around midnight we called a taxi to take Telesfor and Frieda home. There was some excitement in the early morning hours. Evidently Frieda had gotten hysterical in the middle of the night, and Telesfor tried to calm her down with sedatives. Then he came and got my father. They took the new bride to the hospital, where she gradually felt better in the course of the day. The way they put it to us children was "Aunt Frieda got sick last night." But later we learned a different version, a family "rumor" that, until the wedding night of the over-fifty-year-old groom and the ten-years-younger bride who was now married for the second time, Frieda was supposedly still a virgin!

There were many celebrations in 1936. In May, just before the Olympic games, I had my bar mitzvah.

We no longer had the money to have a huge celebration, as is common for bar mitzvahs. The aunts helped us out once again, not only with the party but even with our clothes for the occasion. I got a new suit—light blue, sporty, with knickerbockers. It was really smart. Margot got a dress suit with a three-quarter-length jacket and a new hat. We got new shoes too and looked very spiffy. That afternoon, after the ceremony, all our old friends came to our apartment on Buschallee, even the Hauke and Schulz baker families from Prenzlauer Strasse, with whom my parents used to go to the Pastry-Cooks' Ball.

Some of us went for an hour's drive on the Reich autobahn near Bernau. Werner Schulz, the baker's son, had a new Mercedes. He took my cousin Inge. Margot and I sat in the back of Herr Hauke's car. It was so exciting! We were racing at seventy-five miles per hour while they were getting dinner ready at home.

The whole family, Jews and Christians, a lot of our old friends, everyone all dressed up, a really opulent celebration. It was actually spooky, as if there weren't a Hitler. My bar mitzvah was the last beautiful family event that we celebrated on such a large scale.

One day in the spring of 1936 my teacher took me aside after school and gave me a letter for my parents—perfidiously unsealed. I was shocked and asked what I had done. He tried to calm me down, but the letter said that the school fees for the last three months had to be paid, or else. . . . It was really bitter for my parents. And especially for me! But they could no longer afford the twenty marks per month.

I guess my aunts couldn't afford it either, or maybe my parents were too ashamed to ask them. I had to leave school and find an apprenticeship. Margot had just gone through the same ordeal. We both started apprenticeships in the garment industry. "At least you can earn good money there" was the consolation. Always look on the bright side. . . .

And I did. As a wage-earning apprentice I was suddenly a "grown-up," not a mere schoolboy anymore. So I decided not to take the change so hard.

My father would have liked to find a place for me at Adler's, the Jewish pastry shop and café on the square at Wittenbergplatz. Everyone had always thought that would be a good trade for me, and actually I wouldn't have disagreed. But then we found out there was a new regulation that no foreign Jews were allowed to do an apprenticeship in the food industry.

Through an ad we found a placement for me at Bernhard and Isaak Barkowsky's on Badstrasse in the Wedding district. They made clothing for men, boys, and children. The Barkowsky family consisted of five unbelievably ugly brothers with even uglier wives. Each brother had a clothing store—on Müllerstrasse, Badstrasse, Reinickendorfer Strasse, Landsberger Strasse, and one near Potsdamer Strasse in the Schöneberg district. Every one of them was worth over a million. I started out dusting, folding suits, cleaning up—basic apprentice chores. I earned fifteen marks per month; later it went up to twenty-five. That might not sound like much, but if you think that at that time our apartment cost only about seventy marks per month . . . ! It gave me new self-confidence. Six months later I started working as a salesman for thirty-five marks, and that, of course, was even better.

The years 1936 and 1937 were like a breather for Jews in Germany because of the Olympics. We were left in peace; at least that's how it looked from the outside. The Nazis wanted to keep up appearances.

During preparations for the Olympics, Jews were initially included among the athletes sent to training camps—kept neatly separate from the "Aryans," of course. If achievement had been all that counted, at least half a dozen of them would have been on the German Olympic team. In the end, after a lot of hemming and hawing, two so-called *mischlings*—that is, "half-Jews"—were allowed to participate. One was Helene Mayer, who won a silver medal in women's fencing and accepted it politely with a Nazi salute. Next to her on the victory platform were two Jews, Ilona Schacherer-Elek from Hungary and Ellen Preis from Austria. One of Preis's teammates for track and field was a relative of mine—Walter Beck from Vienna—who won bronze in the ten thousand meters.

I felt content in my Jewish environment. I tried out some of the numerous Jewish youth groups but wasn't able to decide on a particular orientation yet. Besides that, I was still training at Grunewald stadium, did a lot of sports, and continued one or the other little affairs from my school days. That was how I adjusted to my new life situation as gently as possible. I mean, I had been considered a cultured young man, not a salesboy! I had to find a way to make the most of the changes that had been forced upon me.

I think I was pretty successful as a salesman. I scurried about, following the customers around, and was very helpful. The men who shopped at Barkowsky's were all mature and experienced, workers from the Wedding district. I found them exciting—and was constantly measuring their crotches! That wasn't necessary, since the clothes weren't custom-made, but they didn't know, innocent and warmhearted as they were.

It sometimes happened that one of them would laugh and say to me, in a heavy Berlin working-class accent, "Hey there, that's enough of that. I'm not made of stone, you know!" But it was never angry. If someone had ever tried to touch their behinds, they probably would have blown up, but I never did that. But in the front . . . well, they liked that.

Some of them would want to try on a pair of pants, and when I'd hand the trousers in to the fitting room, they weren't wearing underwear. So I'd get a good look. "But you aren't allowed to try things on without underwear." "Oh, come on . . . it'll just be a second. . . ." "Well, okay."

In a word, they liked me. You have to imagine, I was a little blond squirt selling leather coats for 120 marks—back then that was a small fortune for a working-class man. The least expensive pants cost 295! I would never have let myself be helped by a greenhorn like me.

Good old Uncle Paul took on a new role for me around this time. I had two hours for lunch, and the store wasn't far from Aunt Anna and Uncle Paul's. "Of course the boy will come to us every day and eat lunch with us!" they decided.

There was always an incredible amount to eat at their place. They devoured quite a bit themselves. Uncle Paul loved lard sandwiches with herring, and when Aunt Anna wanted to tease her husband, she'd say that he sometimes put chocolate on top. But she wasn't any better. I had no complaints, and besides, it meant quite a savings for my parents.

I sort of switched to Uncle Paul's family. It went pretty far. I don't know what Aunt Anna thought of it all, but she was the one who said, "Come on and take a nap after lunch. Paul has already lain down." So I snuggled up next to him on the couch. We basically did it every day, without taking off our clothes, of course, but then we had a long history of exchanging discreet affection. "Oh, how sweet they look lying there together! Isn't it nice that the boy comes to us all the time, Paul?"

While I was at the Jewish School, I had become a member of the Jewish Kulturbund, or Cultural League. It became more and more important for us from the mid-1930s on, since Jews were increasingly excluded from "Aryan" cultural institutions—both as artists and audience.

Aside from theater evenings, classical music was performed, sometimes with a full orchestra, sometimes with a chamber orchestra. They had operettas, dance performances, films, and literary readings, and in the afternoons there was a special youth program. The artistic quality was definitely competitive. For example, Jewish performers from Hungary, which had not yet been occupied at the time, were given engagements. But most of all there were first-class artists from Germany who were not allowed to perform anywhere else anymore.

During the 1937–38 season, the Cultural League was at its peak. In Berlin alone there were 17,500 members. A lot of "Aryan" artists came to the premieres too, to see what the Jews were doing. I hardly missed a single performance, often attending with Margot. At the same time, Cousin Inge took me to the "Aryan" theaters—the Deutsches Theater, for instance—so I could even make a comparison.

Until 1939–40 the Cultural League tried to offer a sort of general education in the artistic sphere. This cultural program had special meaning for the audience, since it was also a proud and confident expression of our Jewish identity. An extension and culmination—and certainly to some extent a perversion—of this relationship to art was the Jewish cabarets that developed later in some of the Eastern European ghettos. Of course, these should not be confused with the girls' orchestras in Auschwitz-Birkenau or Theresienstadt, in which the musicians were forced to perform by the Nazis. There, art was brutally forced out of the performers and by no means represented an assertive expression of life and dignity "in spite of everything."

As long as it was still possible to emigrate, the Cultural League tried to place its artists abroad. As late as 1940, for example, it still advertised in Shanghai newspapers, offering a trio, a jazz combo, and a chamber orchestra. And it was sometimes successful! So musicians could still leave Germany to form new groups in Shanghai. Jewish cultural life remained active until the very last second. In September 1941 the Jewish Cultural League was disbanded by the Nazis, and after that cultural events only took place illegally.

In Berlin during 1936 and 1937, the Cultural League evenings were special occasions. One time my mother and two of the aunts stitched and sewed for a whole afternoon because Margot needed something new to wear for the evening's premiere!

My sister worked in the women's clothing industry, and my mother had to start earning money as well. Our cousin Inge worked as a photograph retoucher for a Jewish man on Friedrichstrasse, not far from the S-Bahn station. She earned good money and always had a lot of work, so she suggested that my mother take on some of her orders. She'd come to us at home and teach my mother the basic skills, and soon she brought my mother a pile of photographs to retouch at home. My mother was never very good at it, Inge confided to me later. Since she didn't have a permanent position she got less money, of course, but we needed the supplementary income, no matter how little.

In 1937 Inge bought a canoe, and sometimes she took us to a lake near Hohen Neuendorf on the weekends, where Frau Pape, her aunt, had a house. My cousin's boat was named *Kerlchen,* or "Little Fellow." She never thought much of men; the boat was enough masculinity for her. That's why she never had any steady companion, and that's why we could come along. Good thing my mother could sew or alter her dresses and coats to fit the hump on her back, as it was constantly getting bigger.

Since she had a nice soprano voice, Inge took singing lessons from Margret Pfahl, a half-Jewish singer from the Charlottenburg Opera. She wanted to become a "serious" German singer, not a creature like her mother, who had had affairs with Jewish singers and actors. She had made it as far as the chorus, but at some point her hunchback really did get in the way—not only visually, but in terms of her singing and breathing ability. It really was detrimental to that.

When my mother got together with Inge about the retouching work, they would talk about singing as well. Sometimes Inge would sing something for us; later we tried singing duets. I learned about opera music from her. Even earlier I could read music, although not very well. Now I became her singing coach, but not on the piano. My voice evolved into a tenor, and I would sing the corresponding part. If she sang the role of Mimì from *La Bohème,* I did Rodolfo. And my mother listened with tears in her eyes.

All my cousins became staunch Nazi women. They experienced Nazi Germany as something new, developing, something they could help build, and they wanted to be part of it. I guess Inge got it through her father, Pape, the actor. For the time being, she made a gracious exception for us. "Well, if all Jews were like you. . . ." There were loads of Nazis like that. They nurtured their anti-Semitic prejudice, totally unimpressed by the fact that their concrete experiences with Jews were totally different from all the clichés. My cousins simply stopped visiting us at some point, but they also never did anything that directly hurt us.

3

SUDDENLY OUR WORLD COLLAPSED. On March 12, 1938, German troups invaded Austria. The people cheered and the world ignored it. A good two weeks later—it was a Friday—we got an official letter.

We had to vacate our apartment in Weissensee by April 1; we had four days. We were no longer Austrians, since Austria no longer existed. But we didn't become German citizens either. Now we were just Jews.

What was to become of us? First of all, it was clear that our big apartment was gone. And second, we were sent back to the district we came from—the Scheunenviertel. We were supposed to find some place to stay there in a so-called *Judenhaus,* a "Jews' house."

My father was absolutely devastated. He viewed Germany as his homeland, the country he admired. And now this country didn't want him as a citizen. He barricaded himself in the bedroom and didn't come out for days. We contacted Wobbi, who promised to help us with the move by arranging a truck, cartons, and workers to do the carrying. But of course, he didn't happen to have an apartment in the Scheunenviertel to offer.

It was as if my parents were paralyzed. On Sunday I went to the Jewish Community offices on Oranienburger Strasse. We had forty-eight hours until the eviction. During those two days, I dragged my mother around to look at at least fifteen rooms we could have sublet. Each one was worse than the previous one.

In one case I would have had to share a room with the son of the family and Margot would have had to share with our parents—that's how inviting the possibilities were. I didn't like the boy very much; he was fat, so I protested. In another apartment there was an old woman in the middle of the living room sitting on a chamber pot making loud noises—Cheers! Bon appetit! This lady had two sons who slept together in a wide bed. With

32

grins as broad as the bed they said to me, "You can join us." That scared my mother.

Last but not least—my mother had already given up—the woman from the Jewish Community office had given me another address. It was number 12a on Prenzlauer Strasse, where we used to live. Our old house was number 46, right across the street. An old friend of ours lived there, good old Frau Szczepanski, the Polish building superintendent's wife. There were Jews living in all three apartments facing the street. They were forced to take in additional Jews since the apartments were so spacious.

Frau Szczepanski greeted me at the top of her lungs, "Hey, son!" I ran over to her and showed her the form with which we could be assigned to one of the apartments. "Leave it to me!" she said. The landlord was an "Aryan," but since he owned this "Jews' house," he had to give his approval. She took care of it in no time, and I went back to our apartment in Weissensee triumphant.

"We have an apartment!" I announced to my mother. "Where?" came the breathless question. It was just like when someone has a baby and asks, "Boy or girl?" I answered, "You won't believe it! In Frau Szczepanski's building!"

My father heard that and locked himself in his bedroom again. He felt like a failure! He should have arranged the apartment, not his fifteen-year-old son. That was the first "mission" I successfully handled on my own. I had learned something. We had been stripped of my father's citizenship. Through my Christian mother we still had a connection to the "Aryans," but in a crisis situation they wouldn't be able to help us either. It was time for me to start taking on more responsibility.

After my parents had given away a pile of furniture, we moved in with a young couple, Erich and Edith Nehlhans. He was president of the oldest synagogue in Berlin, on Heidereutergasse. He was a pious man with a lively, somewhat less pious wife. They loved each other a lot. And often. After all, they were young. We became friends quickly. I can still hear Aunt Anna saying, "You're always so lucky! Right away you meet such charming people!"

Basically, that was a typical reaction. They never said a word about the atrocity that we were robbed of our citizenship and our apartment by the despotic oppression of the Nazis.

The Scheunenviertel was looked down upon by many "Aryans" and even by the assimilated and wealthy Jews. They found it untenable, insulting, full of clichés, and an embarrassment. In the 1930s it didn't even look all that Eastern European anymore—as if all the men walked down the street with *peyes*, with sidecurls! And so what if they did!? They wore caftans and hats. That was enough to horrify the parvenus in the western part of the city. Those of us who were less well-to-do had nothing to do with the Charlottenburgers—if I could avoid it, I never went west of Brandenburg Gate.

Here in the Scheunenviertel many of the people felt German too—among them, my father—but it didn't make them arrogant. When we moved to Weissensee in 1927 it certainly represented a social step up, but to be honest the modern housing complex in Weissensee wasn't all that classy either. It was a rather left-wing to Communist neighborhood with simple, low-income housing. The hygienic conditions there were better than in the bug-infested old apartments in the Scheunenviertel, but that was about the only benefit. My father would never have even thought of trying to find an apartment in the western part of the city. His business partner had a villa in the Grunewald forest, which, among other things, served to swallow up much of the money from their joint business. My father sometimes went there for glittering evening parties, but that was it—like a foreign visitor taking a peek. He didn't feel at home there.

In view of the losses we had experienced and the collapse of our bourgeois world, we regarded our return to the Scheunenviertel in 1938 as something of a relief. After all, we were coming back to a place where we had spent many wonderful years. . . .

Walking through the streets of the Scheunenviertel, nothing had changed much. There were still a lot of Jewish businesses; the synagogue I used to attend was still there on Heidereutergasse. The streets were always full of people. On Shabbos you could see masses of Jews going for walks between Alexanderplatz, Hackescher Markt, and Oranienburger Strasse. The buildings looked pretty much the way they do today, to the extent that they still exist at all. They were not poorly built but were a little rundown—a mixture of apartment buildings and businesses, which displayed some of their wares out on the sidewalks. There were fruit and vegetable stands, butchers, bakers, coal and potato vendors, and in between small workshops, cobblers, tailors, and artisans' shops hidden away in the courtyards and factory lofts. Today, some of the streets in the Kreuzberg district look similar. But in the Scheunenviertel of the late 1930s there were no nice little cafés where you could sit outside; instead, there were corner bars that served snacks. And all over there were lots of kids running around. It was buzzing—urban and alive and not at all fashionable.

We felt comfortable there. Even my mother didn't need long to feel at home again. As always, we tried to make the best of our new situation. That was realistic—who could we have complained to anyway, and with what prospects of being heard?

After we moved, a period of religiousness began for me, thanks to Erich Nehlhans. I started becoming interested in the spiritual side of Judaism. He taught me Jewish rituals; I learned about using *tefillin*, the phylacteries worn by religious Jews, and I started reading the Torah. I went with him to the synagogue on Fridays and Saturdays. My parents, especially my mother, weren't very happy about it, but they didn't dare protest. Once I heard my mother complain to Aunt Trude that at a time when things were getting worse and worse for Jews, her son emphasized his own Jewishness with a sudden interest in religion that exceeded anything our family had ever practiced before.

In 1937–38, Uncle Wobbi built his house in Teltow, south of Berlin. He was a military engineer and thus knew earlier than others that Hitler was preparing for war. So he "prepared" his house. He had special plans for the basement; it was made into an outright air raid shelter. Next to the house there was a garage. Sometime later he made me an offer: "If you and your friends are ever in trouble, then I'll meet you all somewhere and we'll drive into the garage with the car. No one would see. From there, you can enter the basement directly." A hideout. He was already thinking in those terms. There was no question—he was determined not to let the Nazis drive a wedge between the Christians and the Jews in the family.

Uncle Wobbi drove to Vienna with the same determination in 1938, after Hitler annexed Austria. I don't know if he had business to do there anyway or if his sole purpose was to contact the Viennese Becks. In any case, he wanted to find out how they were faring.

Grandfather had already died. Grandmother was half crazy and had started becoming a risk—she'd go running through the streets screaming, "You damned Nazis!" and stuff like that. Surprisingly enough, no one in the family had even made the slightest attempt to leave the country. They all ended up being murdered in concentration camps. Only one cousin of mine survived and returned to Vienna. In the 1970s he told me, "You cannot imagine what it meant to us that Uncle Wobbi came to Vienna in 1938. This Christian from Berlin, a military engineer, showed us how the family was sticking together!" Uncle Wobbi moved freely throughout the city. He went to the theater and to cafés and restaurants, and he always brought the relatives with him. They told him that it was perhaps not a good idea for them as Jews to go here or there, but Wobbi insisted, "If you are there with me, nothing will happen!" And nothing did.

Like many others, my parents did not start thinking about emigration until 1938, and by then it was already much too late. As non-Zionists they would have preferred to go to the United States; that country seemed the most civilized. My father went to the Jüdischer Hilfsverein, the Jewish Aid Association, where you had to stand in line for days just to get information. It was hopeless. We had no chance: no money, no special papers, no one who could apply for an affidavit to vouch for us, nothing of the sort. We were just a poor family from the Scheunenviertel that was not in a position to buy the tolerance of another country.

Actually, we were not all that despondent when my father confirmed what we had secretly suspected all along. Emigration was generally possible only for the rich or for Zionist zealots. We would have to continue to endure life in Germany.

There was possibly one small chance for Margot. As a so-called *mischling*, or "child of mixed blood," she could be sent to England as an au pair through the Quakers. In 1938 we started making arrangements and finally got word that she would be allowed to enter England in the fall of 1939 to take on a position in Birmingham. But then the war started, and Margot too had to remain in Germany.

W E WERE SITTING TOGETHER AT DINNER, my parents, Margot, and me. All of a sudden there was a soft knock at the door, and Erich Nehlhans came in. Usually so elegant, he looked ragged and dirty, and he was more thoughtful and quiet than normally. "The Nazis have done something terrible," he said. "They came into the temple and wreaked havoc. I don't know how much was destroyed, but the building itself is still standing. I heard it's happening all over!"

It was the evening of November 9, 1938. Rioting hordes had stormed the synagogue on Heidereutergasse, but since part of the building had recently been leased to the Post Office, the police came and intervened. After all, the offices of the Post Office had to be protected. So "only" the main room of the synagogue was destroyed. The temple could still be used for services; I personally continued going there until the early 1940s. We simply used the smaller room. Erich Nehlhans was almost calming as he reported this attack by the Nazis, the worst thus far.

The next morning I rode to Barkowsky's, as always. As I was leaving the U-Bahn—the subway—I was seized with horror. All of Badstrasse was destroyed! Later, after the air raids, some of the streets reminded me of how things looked on this fateful day. Until then, I hadn't been aware of which stores belonged to Jews and which didn't. The famous Hemden-Matz men's shirt store, Bata shoes, Etam lingerie, and Salamander with its Jewish manager, here a clothing store, there my Barkowsky's, big and small names—all Jews, all laid to waste.

That night, Nazi thugs had destroyed over 250 synagogues, 7,500 stores, numerous apartment houses, Jewish Community buildings, and cemeteries. Almost one hundred Jews were murdered, hundreds driven to suicide, and thirty-five thousand arrested and carried off.

Barkowsky's shop had a long, narrow salesroom; the clothing hung along the side walls. When I stepped over the glass splinters from the shattered windows and entered the store that morning, all the merchandise was lying on the floor. The elderly salesman I worked with said to me with grim composure, "First clean everything up. Hang it all back up. That isn't half of what we had in storage." But it wasn't all that easy, because the shirts and pants and jackets were all . . . covered with shit! The vandals had thoroughly soiled and smeared everything. As absurd as it sounds, I hung everything up anyway. The stench was gagging.

Then I was sent across to Salamander's. We needed wooden boards to repair the door temporarily and board up the shattered store windows. Since our clothing was delivered in cardboard cartons, we didn't have any. But Salamander had its shoes delivered in wooden crates that could be taken apart. "Go get some wood from your friend across the street!"

He was referring to a small, sturdy apprentice who worked at Salamander's. He was also Jewish and spoke in that typically crude but friendly Berlin manner. He had caught my eye some time before, but unfortunately there was never anything between us. "You need wood? I can give you some," he said and pointed to the shelves. "You know, they were looting like magpies. But they didn't take any pairs, just single shoes. What did they want with them?" We laughed. I packed a few crates under my arm and turned to go. He added, "All the rest they covered in shit. I wanna know one thing: What did the SA eat to shit like that!?"

That's how I experienced the terrible November pogrom that the Nazis called *Reichskristallnacht*. I couldn't join the chorus of voices saying they had seen burning synagogues all over. If all the Jews who say that today had really been standing there watching, then all of German Jewry would have been out on the streets that night. I'm sure whoever happened to be outside ran home as fast as possible as soon as the glass started shattering.

And year after year I observe how the ninth of November is commemorated in Germany, with mayors and dignitaries. They all stand around with dead serious expressions, hanging their heads to the side and looking so sad, you'd think they had lost something. Every year the same words, no matter which party the speakers are from, and all I can do is smell the shit and hear the crude comment of the apprentice.

It was relatively clear what they had "eaten." The pogroms all over had all started at the same time. It couldn't have been a spontaneous "eruption of popular anger," as Goebbels referred to it later. Most of the perpetrators were SA storm troopers; we had gotten to know them as extremely unrefined people from their marches and their attacks against individual Jews. That night they were also drunk as skunks, willing tools of a very calculated oppression that threatened us in its unpredictability. In any case, it was absolutely certain that the Nazis had used Herschel Grynszpan's assassination of the German diplomat Ernst vom Rath in Paris as a pretext to force the Jews out of German economic life once and for all.

A whole series of loyal customers continued to come to Barkowsky's. We boarded up the entire storefront along the street. But it was also possible to enter the shop through the courtyard, where there was a small movie theater. Without batting an eye, the customers would ask, "But now you'll make it a little cheaper, right?" We were able to sell about half of the stock before having a final "clearance sale" in late December—if that's what you want to call it—but doing business wasn't allowed officially.

Countless regulations went into effect over the next few months that made it virtually impossible for Jews in Germany to maintain any semblance of their normal, middle-class lives. Radios, telephones, and valuables were confiscated. We were no longer permitted to run businesses, buy books or newspapers, own motor vehicles, or use public transportation, and times for buying groceries were limited. The Nazis introduced the so-called *Judenbann*, off-limits zones for Jews. That meant Jews were prohibited from using certain streets, public places, and facilities in the city, such as theaters, cinemas, or public bathhouses or swimming pools. Jews who didn't have a Jewish-sounding first name were forced to add either "Sara" or "Israel" to their name; a *J* for *Jude* was stamped in our passports. It was absolutely prohibited for Jews to attend "Aryan" educational institutions, and many Jewish organizations were disbanded. If that weren't enough, the Jews were forced to pay repair costs for all that had been destroyed in the pogrom night; one billion reichsmarks had to be paid to the German government as an "atonement penalty." The Employment Office for Jews was opened in order to regulate where and under what conditions we were still allowed to work.

Erich Nehlhans had built up a small mail-order postcard business over the previous few years. His customers came from the environs of Berlin. Once a year he visited each of them and took their orders, even in 1938. Now he knew he would not be able to travel the following year. To all customers that had ordered, for example, twelve Brandenburg Gate postcards, he sent ten dozen instead of the ordered one dozen, with a letter saying, "I will not be able to deliver to you next year." Most of his customers actually did buy them, stocking up on the cards and paying their invoices. What an easy way to close a business. "Typically Jewish," my mother laughed, not without admiration.

Toward the end of the year, when Barkowsky finally closed his shop, Nehlhans said to me, "Gerhard, I was talking to a cousin of mine recently. He is a representative for a German cardboard packaging factory, and he said, 'Send the kid over sometime; he could be just what we're looking for.'" And that's how I ended up at Alfred Lindau's.

The Lindau Company was my first real job. The pay wasn't great, but at least it was more than I was getting toward the end at Barkowsky's. Cardboard manufacture is a primitive form of factory work, and that corresponded exactly to my coworkers. Most of the people I encountered there seemed slightly feeble-minded and incredibly amoral. Their lives were boring, and so were their jobs. Almost all of them were young people, and they had only one thing on their minds—screwing.

I had to fold or staple the cartons, cut out the slits in the inserts, and the like. Small, trim, and agile, I did my work rather quickly. My coworkers sometimes interrupted their work to watch the little guy. They liked me. Lindau, the boss, was a typical Berliner—friendly and just as simple as his personnel. He lent a strong hand and sometimes even carried the heavy pile of cardboard used to make the cartons himself.

There was one boy there in particular who made an impression on me. His name was Herbert; he was slick and lived for sex alone. He would come to work horny in the morning and announce at the top of his lungs, "Look at this! Today my dick is, once again, uncontrollable!" And whenever he had a chance, he was at it. Four or five girls worked for Lindau, and Herbert badgered more than one of them each day. There was also a lot of fooling around among the men, and when Herbert was in that kind of mood, it was my turn as well.

I felt the same way as the girls; he was too rough for me, and the whole thing was rather unpleasant. At the time I was still pretty inexperienced, and I'm more into caressing anyway. Whenever he'd get his hands on yet another victim on the cardboard stack in the cellar, there were often tears.

That didn't bother him. He knew the men would stick together. It would have been useless to complain. Lindau knew for sure what was going on—whenever he would go downstairs he'd whistle out a warning first—but he never intervened. He might have had a good heart, but he was not very sensitive.

Starting in 1939, the Jews were gradually and systematically turned into slaves of the regime. In Berlin, only half of the prewar population of 160,000 Jews remained at the beginning of the war, and most of them were placed in armaments jobs. They worked hard, trying to better their situation, and were generally well liked among workers and foremen in the factories. Many interpreted their slave labor to be a way of proving that they played an important role for Germany, thus salvaging a bit of dignity and repressing the ever-growing danger as long as possible.

What later became even more obvious had already become apparent: Namely, if Berliners made distinctions, it was generally between social classes and less on racial or ethnic grounds. Solidarity or aid for the oppressed Jews came faster from the simple, underprivileged "Aryans"—even though all social classes of Jews were among the forced laborers.

Our family decided to send my sister to Uncle Wobbi and Aunt Martha in Teltow. They "hired" Margot as a domestic, thus saving her from having to work in armaments. For my sister the new environment was far from pleasant. Living cut off from the big city and her nuclear family made her feel isolated.

Things were different in the "Jews' house" on Prenzlauer Strasse, where everyone knew everything about the neighbors. It must have been like that in olden times, in the ghettos, close and warm and cosy. By being forced together in terms of space, we also grew closer together at a psychological and spiritual level, supporting each other where we could.

Immediately we got to know the Nehlhanses' friends and relatives, and we became a new sort of extended family. I was definitely the driving force behind that. My parents tended to keep more to themselves, but I was a real extrovert. My whole life I have had a way of creating groups and families, provided they liked me and I could offer something, of course. I would never think of expecting someone to love me without my showing that I am deserving of the love by giving something in return.

Maybe it was this new feeling of community and warmth that made World War II seem at first like some venture of the Nazis that had little to do with us—wishful thinking!—and for which they would hopefully have to pay someday.

On that September 1, Frau Szczepanski came racing breathlessly into our apartment at the crack of dawn. "Children, they just announced on the radio"—she still had one—"at five o'clock they will start shooting back; they keep on repeating it. German troops have marched into Poland, my homeland. . . ."

After all the rabble-rousing propaganda against Poland, we were not all that surprised. We didn't start worrying until we realized that the millions of Polish Jews would also be affected—the relatives of the Rosenthal family, for instance, who lived above us. The war did not yet directly change our everyday lives all that much—except for the fact that the Nazis took advantage of the situation to harass us with new prohibitions and regulations, such as the nightly curfew.

A few days later, my old friend Werner Schulz, the baker's son, came by in the evening wearing a full Wehrmacht uniform. He had to go off to war. He got completely plastered at this farewell visit, and in the end he started sobbing, "What have you Jews done to be treated this way?"

The Schulzes, who had been friends with my parents since the 1920s, helped us through to the end of the Nazi period. In 1938 my father decided to give them the family jewelry to take care of. We got it all back in 1945 when we were living in Munich, which cannot be said of all the people asked to act as "take-cAryans." Frau Schulz always sneaked bread and cake to us. The more difficult the times, the more sophisticated the transfer became. For instance, two identical handbags were exchanged, one empty and one full; usually one of our aunts did that for us.

In 1941 old Schulz the baker died, and Werner came over to invite my father to the funeral. Heinrich declined, saying it would probably be better if a Jew didn't show himself there, but the Schulz mother and son insisted: "Of course you'll come, Uncle Heinrich!" That's what they always called him. "We'll pick you up. Leave your yellow star at home. That's just a pile of bullshit! You're among friends." And my father went.

The Christian part of our family had finally grasped the gravity of the situation on November 9. They apparently adopted the principle "Don't let the Jews down!" Nothing was expected anymore from Heinrich Beck and his family—it was just the opposite. Since we didn't have our own apartment anymore, they invited us over more than they used to instead of coming to visit us. But my aunts regularly came to check up on us. They shared cigarettes with us and brought groceries. Whoever bought some sausage, for example, would always put a few slices aside for us and bring them over the next time they visited, as if it were the most natural thing in the world to do. It was hard to accept it at first, but soon we got used to the practice.

There were nevertheless differences. Aunt Trude and Aunt Frieda were afraid, even though their husbands weren't. Trude and Willi only invited us over if other "difficult" guests were there too, such as friends that used to be Communists. Frieda was the target of some cutting remarks from the neighbors—"So, now it's hitting your relatives too!?"—and she got more and more worried. "And what if there happens to be an air raid while you're here and we have to go into the shelter and everyone sees us?" she once asked. Telesfor thought that was ridiculous; he was able to take a stand against her fears, and they ignored the remarks as best they could.

(By the way, those were the same neighbors who in 1938 "acquired" all our china from our apartment in Weissensee, at a giveaway price, of course.)

Martha and Wobbi didn't change the way they treated us at all; the same was true of Anna and Paul. Even after I stopped working for Barkowsky, they still expected me to visit whenever I could—"if only to pick up your weekly allowance!" they would say to the son they never had, much to Cousin Gerda's consternation.

The Krügers had a friend who, though not a member of the Nazi Party, nevertheless had very strong nationalist sentiments. He had pins with the Reich flag and all that stuff. I remember how Anna showed him into the apartment just as I was going from the kitchen to the living room. He took off his jacket and was about to go into the living room when she tapped him on the lapel of his jacket and said, "Friedel, you're not going in there wearing that!" He was startled. "Oh, is Heinrich there? Sorry." And he took the pin off. They demanded some show of respect, in spite of everything.

Gerda made no bones about showing her rejection. Paul invited us to her wedding in 1940, but she was opposed. It wouldn't have bothered her husband-to-be, who was in the Wehrmacht and after the war joined the Social Democratic Party, but Gerda got what she wanted. My father laughed about it; my mother was deeply hurt: "So the Nazis did manage to split up our family after all!"

That was a very typical attitude. From most Germans you could expect a more or less tactful distance at best, like "We don't want anything to do with it." "It" could mean, depending on the situation, either the discrimination against Jews or Jews themselves. After the war an unbelievable number of Christians told me they secretly helped the Jews. If you could count on those "statistics," millions of Jews would have had to have been saved. It was really more their way of saving their own souls. Many had their exceptional "good Jew," a good and pitiable person whom they treated nicely to make it all the more easy to close their eyes to the mass crimes going on against humanity. I don't think anyone was really thinking about "afterwards" at the time. But only in very few cases did this niceness—definitely better than hostility, which was more frequent—turn into real aid. Within our circle of friends and acquaintances, in any case, almost all of them tried not to totally deny the former times, before Jews started getting harassed.

IN EARLY 1940, smart Herr Nehlhans gave me a good idea—possibly a way for me to avoid having to work in the armaments industry. "Listen, boy, have you ever thought of a *hachshara?*" *Hachshara* was the name of the Zionist preparatory and training centers where young people received instruction at no charge prior to emigrating to Palestine. There was a practical, agricultural aspect and a Zionist, spiritual one. Most of the centers were located in the environs of Berlin on farms and estates.

I went to the Palestine Office on Meinekestrasse, near the classy Kurfürstendamm boulevard, and ran into an old acquaintance, Friedel de Vries, who used to be the leader of my Jewish youth group. "Hey, Gerhard, you want to join too! Come back in two weeks; I'll find something for you!" I spoke to Alfred Lindau, who wrote me a great letter of recommendation and wished me luck: "If you find something better, then do it. But you can come back anytime."

A Zionist training center in Germany in 1940, to prepare for emigration? That might sound absurd in view of the genocide of the Jews that was in the offing. But in its historical development, it really was logical.

The *hachshara*—Hebrew for "training"—was a project of the Hechalutz ("pioneer"), the nonpartisan Movement of Zionist Work Pioneers for Palestine, which was founded in Palestine in 1917. The Hechalutz opened its world office in 1921 in Vienna (it was later moved to Geneva). Jews wishing to emigrate had to participate in a *hachshara* for a certain length of time in their home countries, in work houses (in the cities) or on farms (in rural areas). They were basically kibbutzim transplanted to Europe. Starting in 1933 there was a great increase in interest in the Hechalutz in Germany. More and more Jews were applying to make their *aliyah*, to emigrate to Palestine, since a certain immigration quota was guaranteed through the Jewish Agency for Palestine, run by and for Jews which the British mandate in Palestine had authorized. There were over eighty *hachshara* centers as early as 1936 in Germany and the neighboring countries. As of 1938 the German Hechalutz was forced to be subsumed by the Palestine Office, but by no means did it discontinue its programs. By 1941 almost forty thousand young Zionists had gone to Palestine.

Adolf Eichmann, head of the Office for Jewish Matters in the Reich Security Main Office, found the Zionist emigration very convenient, since until around 1941 Nazi policy aimed to drive as many Jews as possible out of Germany. With regard to wealthy Jews, they didn't care where to, provided all their property was confiscated prior to departure; the poor Jews would be sent to Palestine through the Hechalutz, which covered all costs. In 1938 Eichmann took over the direction of the newly formed Reich Central Office for Jewish Emigration in Berlin, which worked together with the compulsory Reich Association of Jews and the Zionist Palestine Office. Similar to later deportation procedures, the idea was to have Jews participate in carrying out what the Nazis had planned for them, of course under Nazi control and direction. Whether the Zionists liked it or not (and of course they didn't like it), Eichmann initially supported the goal of *aliyah* and thus the *hachsharot*. In fact, at the 1961 Eichmann trial, I had to testify in court on this point.

But in 1940 the number of people wanting to immigrate to Palestine far exceeded the quota set by England. And due to the war, the British had stopped all emigration from Germany to Palestine anyway. From 1939 to 1941 illegal immigration attempts still took place. In the spring of 1940 I was sixteen and thus a member of the intermediate *hachshara* group, which included youths between fourteen and eighteen. Because of the limited number of immigration certificates, our group had to wait longer than the adults for permission to make their *aliyah*, but who could afford to wait any "longer" in 1940!?

After the pogroms of November 9, 1938, there were two main developments in Jewish life in Germany. The Nazis had made sure through prohibitions and regulations that very little of the diversity in Jewish institutions remained, and these were subject to strict controls. The successor institution to the independent Reich Representation of Jews in Germany was the Reichsvereinigung, or Reich Association of Jews, on Kantstrasse in Charlottenburg. It was controlled by the Reich Interior Ministry. The Zionist organizations met in 1939 at Meinekestrasse 10: the Palestine Office, the Jewish Jugendhilfe, or Youth Aid, and thus the Youth Aliyah. Independent of the emigration efforts, the Jewish Communities also worked hard to rebuild Jewish life after November 9, facing great difficulties and considerable costs. Synagogues were restored; schools were opened; Jewish cultural activities were subsidized. Their message was: Stay in Germany and, subject to Nazi conditions, make life as good as possible. It was the last remaining notion of German-Jewish assimilation.

Without thinking all too much about it, I took advantage of both alternatives. Just as Margot and I regularly attended services in the synagogue and watched performances at the Jewish Cultural League, I took up the idea of *aliyah*, even though my parents were rather skeptical of Zionism.

Friedel de Vries arranged a place for me at the *hachshara* center in Skaby, east of Königs Wusterhausen, southeast of Berlin. It was a beautiful old farming estate with a German landlord. The Hechalutz had dormitories for the Young Pioneers built on the property. Although it was actually only meant for the older *hachshara* members, I went there in May 1940.

My first chore was to take care of the baby animals, since I was so small and agile. This was supposed to pave my way to a Zionist future? The calves just stare at you. They really are pretty stupid animals, and if you stop moving for a second they shit on your shoes. How exciting.

I would have preferred to spend more time with the others. There were well over a hundred of us in Skaby, and I really enjoyed meeting new friends. Agricultural chores were only done in the mornings; in the afternoons we had classes on Jewish subjects, including religion and Hebrew. And evenings we would become absorbed in Jewish spiritual life, traditions, customs. They were called "social evenings." Since I didn't know any Hebrew, I didn't understand a word of the songs and poems, but it was the same for most of us. Aside from its definitely Zionist orientation, this kibbutz was not tied to any party and accepted young people from all social classes. In view of Eretz Israel, wealth or poverty was secondary. It was here that I got my first information about what Israel was like and was supposed to become. Where were we going anyway, if it worked and we got a place on a ship? What was awaiting us?

Since it was so boring for me with the calves, I started getting more and more interested in the evening events. Finally I was asked to organize something myself. Generally, whoever wanted to get involved in the evening events could do so. I took the text of a beautiful prayer I had learned in the synagogue. The first line goes like this: "*Hashiveinu Adonai eilecha v'nashuva*—Help us to return to You, O God, then truly we shall return."

At sixteen I didn't understand the religious challenge of returning to the righteous path with God's help, but I took the text and interpreted it in a way that corresponded to my picture of the world. God's presence and strength were concepts too strong for me to grasp. My talk stressed two ideas. First, I emphasized a person's freedom of choice. It is not God who demands something of us; instead, we make demands of God. Second, I interpreted "returning" to mean "homecoming," to Palestine, of course. Lead us to Eretz Israel, God, and we shall find the way to our true selves! Any orthodox scholar would shudder at this interpretation, but I still believe in it today. This is my approach to the basic philosophical questions—never high-flown and purely theoretical, but clearly referring to people and their reality.

Then we softly sang a few songs that evening, and no one left the event sad or despondent. That was my first attempt at being a *tarbutnik*, or cultural representative.

I got something else out of that evening as well. After having initially felt a little lonely, since I was one of the youngest there, I met Reuwen. On the Sunday after my *tarbut* evening he invited me to go on an outing with him. Skaby is located in the middle of a forested area, and we just took off hiking. As a city kid, I thought it was absolutely beautiful out there in the country, and romantic too, but this day was something even more special. We discussed the subject of the talk I had given. We talked and talked and got closer to each other—casually, almost inevitably.

Reuwen was a strong, sturdy type, more physical than I was but by no means stupid. With his unobtrusive, reserved manner, he was respected and often asked for his opinion. But he didn't have any close friends in Skaby. Many of the other pioneers were from rural areas, and they were simple, some of them almost vulgar. Although his family was also poor, Reuwen was one of the refined people. He was tender and delicate, and he radiated a longing for hugs and closeness. He was almost a head taller than I was, and a strong "Jewish" nose jutted out from a pretty face. He had dark hair, sparkling black eyes—it was not only his eyes, but his look— and a soft, sensual mouth.

We were sitting under a tree at the edge of a meadow where I tended my calves during the week. At some point he stretched out his hand, and what started out as tenderly getting closer to each other quickly and deliberately turned sexual. Reuwen was without a doubt gay, which is not the case with all the men I have ever had loving encounters with.

The friendship with Reuwen, a romantically surging youthful love, continued throughout my entire stay in Skaby. I thought living there was incredibly erotic anyway—such an unfamiliar closeness to nature for an entire summer—and the other boys! I relished the sight of their beautiful bodies in the group shower after work. They were in their early to mid-twenties, athletic, and—despite the general atmosphere—forward-looking and optimistic. The *hachshara* was like a—no, not a *lonely* island. But it was remote and idyllic, while outside the storm of history was raging. We didn't hear much of what was going on, and it was as if the war didn't affect us at all.

The actual *aliyah* became more and more difficult. In Skaby alone there were 180 *chaverim*, comrades, waiting to emigrate. Actually, I should have completed two years of *hachshara* before being allowed to emigrate. But I received a place on the passenger list anyway, on the *Pacific*, the ship second in line to the Promised Land. I could hardly wait for the day to come. Reuwen and I often fantasized about how our friendship would finally have a chance to blossom once we were free.

One day I suddenly collapsed. It was during the tomato harvest. That might sound idyllic, but it was a terrible grind; those things grow pretty low to the ground, and you have to stand stooped over the whole time. I was admitted to the Jewish Hospital in Berlin with a tear in my stomach wall. I had to stay about three weeks, and while I was there a group from Skaby took off on its way to Palestine—with "my" ship! Ephraim Frank, the Berlin Hechalutz director, accompanied the group, as did a few other prominent figures. Reuwen was among them as well. When we said goodbye, we never suspected that we would not see each other again until many years later in Israel.

The *Pacific* never arrived in Palestine. It wasn't allowed to dock in

Haifa. The British refused to give the passengers entry permits and instead put them aboard another steamer, with the ironic-sounding name *Patria*, destined for Mauritius. In order to prevent the ship's departure, the Haganah, the Jewish underground militia in Palestine and the predecessor to the Israeli army, detonated a bomb designed to make the ship unseaworthy. But the explosion caused more damage than had been planned; the *Patria* sank, and 254 people died. The survivors were accepted a short time later onto existing kibbutzim.

The following seems like a P.S. to my barely missed emigration. In Holon, where I later lived in Israel, the main square in the city was called Struma Square, in commemoration of the *aliyah* ship by that name that sank in the Bosporus in 1942. The message the name conjured up was architecturally incorporated in an almost eerie way: Whenever it rained, the water never drained from the square but literally drowned it.

WHEN IN THE LATE FALL OF 1940 I was released from the hospital, the first thing I had to do was report to the Employment Office for Jews. I reported on my training in Skaby and said that I wanted to return there, since agricultural work was, after all, real work. But they said, "No. According to the files you used to work in a carton factory. We could use you there at the moment."

In the meantime my sister had been protesting vehemently. She couldn't take it any longer in Teltow with the *goyim*. Martha and Wobbi had marital problems that were beginning to get out of hand. My aunt even shot at her husband once, and Margot just wanted to get out of there. So she came back to us and thus also had to go to the employment office. She was sent to Siemens. She didn't care. She'd do anything just to be back home in Berlin.

My father worked for the Reich railroads building tracks and replacing ties; an efficient rail system was needed for the war (and not only for that). He had to perform very hard physical labor—dragging ties, turning huge screwdrivers—outdoors, no matter what the weather. But in fact he was very content. He had an important task to do!

One day he brought my mother a gigantic bottle of French perfume. It was in bad taste but was quite a big deal. One of his foremen had sold it to him under the table. "Look what our soldiers brought with them from Paris!" my father beamed. *Our* soldiers?

Three members of the family were wage-earners. The illusion of a secure existence. One weekend, when my father, sister, and I laid out our pay envelopes on the table, he added it all together and said in all seriousness, "You know what, children, when I still had my business, sometimes I didn't earn as much as we have now!"

He did everything he could to calm us and himself. The big, and expensive, apartment was gone. We could hardly be squeezed into an even smaller space—that could only be coffins! We had work. So everything was taken care of. It seemed as though we could breathe a sigh of relief, for the time being.

My new carton factory, the EPeKo on Herzbergstrasse in the Lichtenberg district, was a huge business—absolutely no comparison to Lindau's small shop. There were long, dimly lit production halls surrounding two courtyards that were always full of trucks. All around were piles of scrap cardboard and packaging materials. The name EPeKo was actually the initials of the two directors: *E* for Erich, who was very personable, almost a real "Jew friend," as they would say; *Pe* for Pröll, who practically always ran around in a uniform, a real Nazi, too stupid to be considered mean; and *Ko* for Company. To watch over the Jewish forced laborers, they had hired a former SA man named Hinrichs, who was disabled. It was said that he'd been shot in the leg in 1934 during the so-called Röhm Putsch—which means he was a hundred percent gay, just like Röhm. Pröll had actually hired him to harass the workers, but Hinrichs couldn't really manage it. A lot of the Jewish workers were incomparably smarter than he was, and it filled him with a certain respect, despite himself.

The Jews, more women than men, worked in the back departments of the factory—the cardboard and carton departments. In front they made corrugated cardboard. Besides "Aryan" German workers, there were also Dutch and French prisoners in compulsory service. They lived in barracks on the factory grounds, sleeping on straw mattresses in primitive and degrading conditions.

Work at EPeKo was piecework. But aside from the fact that everything was terribly dusty, loud, and unhealthy, I could have had it worse. During the meal breaks we got together with other workers, and just as at Lindau's, here too I thought, "Cardboard workers must be especially dumb. Any idiot could do this work; who would choose to work here?" We Jews hurried about very industriously, in order to have good standing. If cartons were necessary for the war effort, then we were necessary! The cartons were used to ship clothing and food. We had strict deadlines and target amounts. One day's production was loaded the next day, and off it went. In 1941 and 1942 there were twenty-one thousand Jews working in the armaments industry in Berlin, ten hours a day, six days a week.

One day during the breakfast break I met Ruth Gomma, who to this day is one of my closest friends. I was sitting there with my sandwich—thanks to the Christian aunts I still had a piece of sausage or cheese on the bread—and said to no one in particular, "Actually, I haven't really earned what

I'm eating today." The woman next to me looked up, scrutinized me, and asked, "How old are you?" "Seventeen." "Hey, you're a smart kid. I'm going to call you Bobby." That was Ruth Gomma. I have no idea why she wanted to call me that. Bobby is a dog's name, but if it made her happy, then okay, Bobby it is. Maybe because she loved to pet and cuddle with me.

Ruth Gomma was fifteen years my senior, a lively, fascinating woman. She had a bobbed haircut and wore a large pair of glasses on her long, oval face; she drew attention to them by always grabbing the frame while looking straight at someone with her critical glance, submitting a thin-lipped judgment. She looked taller and thinner than she really was and had a good figure, which her clothing emphasized superbly. She had previously worked in the fashion industry and had bought herself a pile of clothes before her company was forced to close. The first time I saw her, in the morning before the shift started, Ruth was wearing a fur coat, which wasn't even officially allowed. She'd change her clothes to start work and cover her head with a large yellow scarf wrapped like a turban. Then she'd put on an apron with a large flowered print and comfortable sandals. She transformed herself into—or rather, disguised herself as—a common worker. I was fascinated by how she managed to have groomed hands and manicured fingernails despite the hard work. She often sang current hits as she worked, with a deep alto voice, loud and not always on key, but with zest and ardor. Even then I noticed that she was often in the center of things when talking to others, whether men or women.

We got along well with our "proletAryan" coworkers. Most of them were women, since the men had all gone to war. Those who worked with us in the Jewish department felt like they were in particularly good company. Ruth Gomma was once talking with an "Aryan" worker who had not a tooth left in her mouth. "Doesn't that bother your husband?" The woman answered innocently, "Ah, that's what he 'specially likes!" The refined Frau Gomma often gave her a bar of soap or some perfume. Tensions developed only rarely, when some of the Jews worked particularly well or fast. Star pupils are never liked much.

After a few weeks I started calling Ruth "Mamsi." I say this without wanting to disparage my mother: Ruth gave me what she never could. With Mamsi, for example, I could talk about intimate things that were on my mind and she understood exactly. She was totally unsentimental and almost sarcastic about affairs of the heart, but that was precisely what I liked. I literally forced her to get to know my first big love. That would never have been possible with my mother. She would have simply said, "Oh, that's just your imagination!" And that's how it was with a lot of things. Mamsi was cultured in a way I wasn't but hoped to achieve someday.

She lived with her Christian mother in a two-room apartment. According to the absurd racial laws of the Nazis, although also a *mischling,* she was safer than Margot and myself, since her Jewish father was no longer living. He had worked at the Volksbühne theater, and their apartment was filled with piles of old theater programs, including one from the premiere of *The Threepenny Opera.* I found it all absolutely fascinating. I went to visit her and got along great with her mother too, right from the start.

Mamsi came to visit us just as often—for instance, on my twenty-first birthday in 1944. This attractive woman gave me . . . two pair of underwear she had sewn herself. That alone would have been enough to shock my aunts terribly, but on top of that they were made of silk! As I unpacked them, my aunts looked away, embarrassed. Typical Mamsi: She had simply taken two of her slips and altered them a bit. They were supposed to make me seductive, but we'll get to that later.

At EPeKo I met a lot of other people besides Mamsi whom I probably would otherwise never have met so early in my life. They helped me forget how terrible it really was to be forced to work there. There was an inspiring painter named Salomon, a former millionaire and owner of a weapons factory in the Rhine region, and Regina Jonas, the only female rabbi in Berlin. Even the poet Gertrud Kolmar worked there. Once I heard her say something that most likely went for many of us there: "Actually I feel more at home here in the factory than at home in my apartment." The rest of the group that was forming were ordinary people—a waiter, a cobbler, a butcher, an undertaker. It was quite a diverse mixture of people who met among the dirt and noise of the production and helped keep the German war machine moving.

It was there that I met Erwin Tischauer, a strong young Jewish man with dark curly hair. He was primarily responsible for the maintenance of the machinery. During the breaks he didn't join the others at one of the "men's tables" but sat off to the side reading. Erwin was considered somewhat arrogant, probably because he was an intellectual. He had studied medicine and dreamed of becoming a surgeon. I told him about my *hachshara,* and he looked up. "Then we must have met. I gave first aid classes at some of the training camps." But I didn't remember him.

After work, when the machines stood silent, he regularly had to lie down inside the cutting machine to clean and oil it. He always stripped himself naked for the task. It was certainly not only because it was absolutely filthy, greasy work, with all the oil and dust. I think he had an almost sensual relationship to the sharp cutting blades. The surgeon-to-be literally lay down "under the knife." Incidentally, until a few years ago he practiced in New York City. His muscular, athletic body looked very inviting; I would have loved to jump right on top of him. And Hinrichs the SA man cast an eye on him as well.

But Erwin did not only interest me in an erotic way. He led a Hechalutz group that met regularly in Berlin and introduced me to the group. Through him I got to know Zionist life in the city. It was flourishing despite the regulation prohibiting Jews from assembling.

Around 1900, Jewish youth associations comparable to the German Youth Movement had started forming with the goal of offering a new sense of community as an alternative to the "unnatural," materialistic, bourgeois lifestyle of the adults. Hiking and outings, sports and singing, Jewish values and traditions all combined into a Boy and Girl Scout–like variant of what I had gotten to know on the *hachshara*. From 1940 on, the only groups that still existed were the illegal Zionist-oriented ones. All the other assimilatory or even German-nationalist Jewish groups had long since disappeared or been disbanded.

I met a central, brilliant figure in the Zionist youth movement. Jizchak Schwersenz was a youth leader, eight years older than myself. He worked in the Berlin Aliyah School at number 74 Choriner Strasse. Schwersenz was made school director once the war started. The Zionist-oriented Youth Aid and the religious Jewish Community, which could hardly be regarded as Zionist, ran the school together, which produced quite a few ideological conflicts. When I saw Schwersenz for the first time with his kids, I heard how they spoke fluent Hebrew with each other and was incredibly impressed. In Skaby only a small minority could speak Hebrew. His intellectual authority fascinated me, but I never really got along with him very well personally, and there were two reasons for that.

I couldn't stand the whole bombastic movement thing with its lofty slogans and banner-waving and marching. It had been officially prohibited since the end of 1934 for Jews to march, go on field trips or sleep over anywhere as a group, wear uniforms, etc. These outward appearances are nothing specifically Zionist, but Jizchak loved them. It was also his idea to make our first names Hebrew—Gerhard became Gad, and Margot became Miriam, etc.—and I did like that. But other than that, the big hoo-ha he made was not my thing. I thrive on familylike group structures, joint work, a feeling of belonging, but I think all that develops through the people themselves and what they are doing, not through external symbols and rituals.

That was *my* reservation. The other one came from him, even if it remained unspoken. Erwin had warned me from the very beginning: "Watch out for him, Gad, he likes boys." As if I had to be warned of that! Jizchak looked great and had a self-assured, winning aura about him. To me he was more distant; I was a little too blunt for him. As a teacher, he considered his position of authority toward his students equally as important as personal closeness; that's how he stimulated their enthusiasm for the common goal.

He was very open and trusting with the boys. Sometimes he would take one of them aside and whisper to him. He really did love them, and they idolized him. On trips and outings there were constantly moments of closeness. If he had gotten to be particularly good friends with one of the boys, the others heard about it immediately. Sometimes it went so far as to cause jealous dramas.

When I got to know Jizchak Schwersenz there were still about ten Zionist groups in the city. Each one had about twenty members, both boys and girls. It was possible to join more than one at a time. I really liked the chance to get to know so many new people and new things. The work we did in the groups was a continuation of what I knew from Skaby: political education, practical and theoretical preparation for emigration to Palestine, Hebrew, Jewish culture, literature, music, philosophy. Erwin also brought me to a group that focused on cultural and artistic work and was politically clearly left-wing, both of which I liked a lot. That group was led by Sonja Okun, a beautiful woman from the Youth Aid leadership who was known for her active love life. Some of the people from the Baum group, a Jewish-Communist resistance group, had originally been part of her circle. The groups usually met privately, at the homes of some of the members, on the weekends or evenings after work.

But Supervisor Hinrichs kept on detailing me for overtime, so I often had to miss the meetings. Some cartons supposedly had to be finished that very evening, urgent shipments for the war effort! Yeah, right! When I was standing at a machine stapling cartons together, he would always sit down next to me and help by putting on the lids. That way he could be near me and observe me. I often wore short pants and a thin shirt. . . . Mamsi said that someday he would attack me. But he didn't.

Then one time he invited me to his home on a Sunday. "I have a few books I'd like to give you," he said, "since you're not allowed to buy them anymore." I talked about it with Erwin. He said, "He has already invited me over a few times too. It'd be better not to go." And I didn't, mostly because I had more important things to do, and I had a funny feeling about it. He had given Erwin *Kampf um Rom* (The Battle of Rome). Now that's an exciting book—fascist crap. He would have to do better than that to tempt me.

When I arrived in the factory on Monday morning, there was a note hanging in the breakfast room. Short and to the point, it said: "Herr Hinrichs died yesterday." He had shot himself in his apartment. I tried to imagine what could have happened. Would he have shot me too? Take one Jew with him to his death? And would he have forced me to have sex with him beforehand? Who knows? Or else I might have discovered the corpse. I didn't even want to imagine what kind of difficulties that could have brought me.

In Erwin's group we were preparing a theatrical reading of Schiller's *Don Carlos*. Goes to show that we certainly didn't only choose Hebrew or Jewish authors. We weren't so stupid as to think that Judaism was the absolute epicenter of the intellectual or cultural world. So we chose Schiller. The roles fit each of us as though they had been written with us in mind. Erwin played the king; his pretty sister was the queen. My sister was Eboli, a certain Manfred Lewin was Carlos, and I was the Marquis Posa. And how could things have gone any other way: Carlos and Posa fell in love. After the passionate crush on Reuwen, Manfred was my first big love.

I didn't really even notice him at first. When he was chosen to play the role of Carlos I was skeptical. He stuttered a little when he read and didn't seem very sure of himself as an actor. He was medium height, strong and athletic, with soft brownish eyes and brown wavy hair that was sometimes messy in a cute way. His lips weren't especially pretty, but full. None of his individual features were all that beautiful; in general he gave a soft and somewhat awkward impression. But he could also be rather spirited. Then the words would just tumble out of his mouth. He would get worked up about our work, Zionism, our message and our goals. The bond between us developed first at an intellectual level.

We rehearsed using the small beige booklets put out by the Reclam publishers. We scribbled all over them with notes and underlining till they bordered on the illegible. Once there was something he couldn't read, so he leaned over my shoulder. I felt his breath on the back of my neck, pleasantly prickling and warm. I caught myself thinking, Yes, stay right there in that position. . . . Something sparked in me.

We started getting together more often to rehearse. I immersed myself deeper and deeper in the character of Posa. It's no wonder we fell in love. I think these two roles are definitely gay. This effusive, typical "oh!" of Schiller's—it couldn't be gayer. When Don Carlos and Posa appear on a stage, there is no doubt that they are a couple in love. Whoever doesn't see that just doesn't want to see it. Manfred and I took it a bit further than how Schiller wrote it.

But first I had to woo him. There were so many people all around Manfred—his large family, the group, diverse activities—that I had the feeling he was out of reach. My only chance was in the play. I knew exactly what I wanted; I wanted to go to bed with him.

And then it happened, after our group meeting one night, on the roof of the building of the former Jewish teachers' association, on Artillerie-strasse. We were camping up there the whole weekend. We had packed food, sleeping bags, a guitar. It was the only alternative we had to a "field trip," since we were no longer allowed to go on outings outside of Berlin. Miriam and I sang two-part harmonies—beautiful, melancholic, kitschy songs; Brahms; Russian songs of the steppes; "No one loves you as I do." It was really too much. But we weren't all that bad. Miriam had a nice voice, even though she couldn't quite hit the higher notes. So she often took the lower voice, and I took the soprano. In the end it must have sounded pretty good, because it led to success with Manfred. He told me later that I had seemed like a girl.

After the music we went to bed—girls in one corner and boys in the other. I had evidently aroused Manfred with my "feminine" charm, be-cause he took the initiative. I knew that that was the only way to get him. I was capable of winning someone over and taking control, but with Man-fred I played the expectant, devoted woman, at least in the beginning. We were very loving with each other. Kissing was especially important to him, but he probably concentrated at first on our shared Zionist spirit, letting this common ground carry him into something physical. Whatever we did, it was not much like gay sex as one thinks of it today, but then again, Manfred was heterosexual anyway. With him, as with many of the lovers my age with whom I had relations during my youth, it was more about joy and fun and sharing hugs and caresses—to feel that the other person was just as aroused as you were. I was so happy that my erotic fantasies with him were satisfied. But he was shocked—at himself. "What have I done?" I would have liked to answer simply, "Just the right thing!"

W E NEEDED WEEKS, even months, until Manfred felt okay about himself. Long, deep, heavy conversations, feelings of guilt, "We can't see each other anymore, especially not at night," and then we would indeed get together again and the conversations con-tinued. Finally I suggested that we just wait and see what happened. Either we would "indulge in our weakness," as he called it, or we would see each other and be able to abstain. Both scenarios would give us some kind of clarity. I just couldn't stand endlessly talking about it anymore. And of course, I was absolutely certain how things would progress.

The group often met at Manfred's place. The Lewin family also lived in the Scheunenviertel, on Dragonerstrasse. There were seven of them in three little rooms. The five children all participated in our groups. Schlomo, the oldest, was at a *hachshara*. I came and went at the Lewins' and finally really got to know all the ins and outs of the neighborhood.

Mother Lewin had her own sources for getting groceries—to supplement the insufficient "Jewish food ration cards"—and shared her connections with my mother. It was mostly dubious stuff, like small, horrendous-smelling pieces of fish, but better than we could get on our own. Finally my mother decided to get past all her reservations; she went to the musty apartment building and got this or that from Frau Lewin.

Manfred's father was a barber for Jews and thus had a profession that was secure in times of crisis. We held our meetings in the same room where he attended to his customers, and Manfred slept there too, in a corner separated off by a frosted glass window. Due to the nightly curfew, there was nothing more natural than my often spending the night at Manfred's, in his bed in fact. His parents were very generous. Space was very tight, and the beds weren't the cleanest either. They didn't bother themselves about who was sleeping in them. For Manfred and me, these nights were our "test." And very soon it became clear that we couldn't and didn't want to abstain. We "indulged" profusely, and finally Manfred managed to work things through with himself and admit his love: "With you it's okay!" I can still vividly remember, it was around my birthday, at the end of June—and the best present I could imagine.

Of course, his parents and siblings noticed our relationship, but it didn't have to be talked about. We were friends, and his parents didn't really want to know the details. They were happy when their children were doing well, when they weren't lonely, when they seemed happy. Anyway, there really were other things to worry about.

We also hosted Hechalutz meetings in our apartment, but not all that often. My father didn't really feel good about it. He could accept the *hachshara* in Skaby because it was legal. My illegal "Zionist activities" in Berlin were something very different. Once I invited Erwin's group and a bunch of *chaverim* from the *hachshara* in Neuendorf to celebrate Bialik's and Herzl's birthdays on May 2. Even Jizchak came. And that meant the scout hullabaloo came too, the whole shebang—drills, clicking heels, salutes. For him it had nothing to do with Prussian or Nazi precision. Drills like that were always common in the youth movement. It drove my father crazy. After the nearly thirty people had finally all gone home, he charged furiously into my room, tore the portraits of the two Zionist leaders from the wall, and cut them up with scissors. "As long as you have a Christian mother—who protects us, don't you forget—you will not worship these Zionist idols!" I acted as though it didn't faze me, but then Frau Szczepanski reinforced his worries the next day. She took him aside and said, "I know that a Jewish underground group is forming up there in your place, but watch out and make sure they don't all go down the stairs at the same time. It attracts attention!"

Theodor Herzl's portrait made trouble for me in another way as well.

There were millions of bedbugs all over the building the Lewins lived in. I think it was the central bedbug office for all of the Scheunenviertel! And the picture of Theodor Herzl that hung in the apartment over Manfred's bed must have served as the main headquarters. I suppose you can get used to anything if you have to. We were lying in bed naked, and the creatures were happily strolling back and forth between us and over us. Sometimes Manfred would stand up, take the picture off the wall, and stick it in a pail of water. Then you could really see them—hundreds swimming around! It seems they liked Herzl. Zionist bedbugs. I encountered the bugs again in Israel. I guess they made their *aliyah*.

Our love had lasted through its first summer. Manfred and I were a couple; all our friends knew. I made sure that Mamsi met him too. One morning, after an air raid patrol, I dragged him with me onto the U-Bahn that Mamsi took to Lichtenberg, so the two of them would meet. The fact that she liked him immediately made me feel all the more in love and helped me forget all the many problems.

Strangely enough, I never doubted our feelings for a second. Even later, I often had relationships with men who were actually straight, for whom I was the only man they ever had anything with. Manfred wanted me as much as I wanted him, and that was all the commitment I needed. He would certainly have become a father of six children if he had survived. Maybe back then we had a different conception of masculinity, but the kind of men called drag queens today, who certainly also existed back then, never attracted me much. My preference for youthful, athletic types—it's really just a matter of taste—made it easy for me. The kind of guy that excited me was all around. I never felt like an outsider because of my homosexuality. We were all united by a strong sense of solidarity. We were oppressed and persecuted, and we had no desire to become people who discriminated against others.

The Nazi pressure entered a new, more severe phase in the fall of 1941. The Jewish youth leadership found out that deportations of Jews were to begin shortly from Berlin, as they had already started in other areas of the Reich. The official Nazi terminology was "migration" or "evacuation" to "work camps" in the east. Step by step the last Jewish institutions were dissolved: the Youth Aid, the remaining Hechalutz facilities, the classes in the Youth Aliyah School. All that was left were the controlled Reich Association of Jews and the politically relatively inconsequential Jewish Community.

The authorities forced more and more now-unemployed teachers and preschool educators into "auxiliary services"—for example, to serve as *ordners,* or marshals, for the deportations that were beginning. Young people fourteen or older had to complete their "labor service" in factories. Alfred Selbiger, who had been the director of the Youth Aid since 1940, was made director of the Jewish Youth Labor Service. The *hachshara* kibbutzim that still existed were converted into "labor service camps."

In late September 1941, right on time for Yom Kippur, the official Jewish Community was told by the Gestapo to convert the synagogue on Levetzowstrasse into a predeportation assembly camp for one thousand people, in anticipation of the "evacuation" of residences needed by the "Aryan" population; that meant organizing personnel, food, medication, and beds. This measure was part of preparations for the overall plan for the "final solution of the Jewish question," which the Nazi Party had resolved at the end of July. In October the first "transport" started rolling from the Grunewald freight depot toward the east, destination Lodz, in Poland.

On September 1 the wearing of the yellow star with the inscription *Jude* was made compulsory for all Jews six years of age and older. We were supposed to pick up the star patches, at first four per person, at a central office of the Jewish Community. We had to pay for them, and they were not cheap! Faced with this situation, the main thing I felt—typical—was a sense of community among us who were affected by this inconceivable measure. For the still very fashion-conscious Mamsi, the world had collapsed. She tried however she could to cover up the hated patch with scarves and fur collars.

At home, as well, the yellow star caused quite a commotion. My mother, who had become Jewish when she converted before getting married, was also required to wear the star, and at first she did. But then her sisters got involved: "Hedie, you've got to do something! You don't have to wear that thing!" They were right. The Nazis made racial distinctions, and according to them my mother was not a Jew. After a few weeks, during which the wheels of the Prussian bureaucracy continued to turn, Hedwig Beck was retroactively excluded from the requirement to wear the yellow star.

When I took the U-Bahn to go to EPeKo—we were still allowed to use public transportation to travel to and from work—I noticed how some people would shake their heads or smile at me. I never experienced any malicious reactions to the yellow star. Certainly other people had different experiences; I guess I was lucky.

In 1941 all public buildings in Berlin had to have air raid patrols. That also applied to the Jewish facilities that had been closed, and Jews were supposed to do those patrols. They were done in groups of two or three. I signed up to do the air raid patrol in the former Youth Aliyah School on Choriner Strasse, which had been damaged by a bomb early that summer, and went with Manfred. In the basement there was nothing but a cot, and we would snuggle up against each other in the dark and forget everything around us for a few hours. It was basically my only chance to be alone with him.

It was around this time that Manfred wrote a little booklet, which he gave to me. It was like a diary, with text and drawings. Manfred kept a record of how we met, little things we did in the group, how we always laughed about Erwin and his dirty fingernails, and small moments from our work on *Don Carlos*. It ended with a poem for me; it wasn't the greatest, but that doesn't matter. He had rhymed "our friendship band" with "in a different land." The message was clear: Should we be torn apart some day, we could still count on our love and would always hear each other's call for help. His poem moves me to this day.

The Berlin Hechalutz groups went through a change in the course of 1941. For one thing, numerous Jewish youths came to Berlin from all corners of the Reich and sought contact with us; second, we responded to the growing pressure around us by intensifying our Zionist zeal.

I started taking on more and more leadership functions. Such development was rooted in the principles of the Free Youth Movement; the leaders train those around them to later assume the leadership positions. Anyone who proved capable would be sent to other groups to gather experience and exchange information. I was constantly on the move, got to know a lot of people, and moved up in all areas of the group work: Zionism, literature, history, Hebrew, whatever.

Erwin was somewhat uneasy with my progress. He didn't quite know if I would become competition for him someday. I would never have dreamed of doing that, but before any difficulties could develop, he withdrew from the Hechalutz work. Lotte Kaiser took over his group. She was one of the prime figures in the youth leadership, and I quickly became friends with her.

I liked her as a woman! That didn't really happen all too often. Maybe it had something to do with her dimples—I often find people with dimples irresistible—or perhaps it was because she seemed austere and masculine. Her autonomy and the liveliness with which she undertook her work impressed me, and I spent quite a bit of time with her. Even though she had a steady boyfriend, Aaron Menczer, who was active in the Jewish youth leadership in Vienna, we even went so far as kisses on the doorstep.

But it was another girlfriend, whom I also met that year, who was later considered my fiancée—Karla Wagenberg. She was at the *hachshara* center in Neuendorf, near Fürstenwalde, and her work brought her regularly to the Hechalutz in Berlin. She turned up in various groups that I was also involved in. As far as appearances were concerned, she was the absolute opposite of Lotte. She was small and round in a typically feminine way; in other words, she was plump. Under a dark bobbed haircut, she had a curious facial expression. Whenever she was about to say something, she would first draw her mouth down at an angle in an affected way. It drove me nuts, actually, and on top of that, her voice was slightly squeaky. Her parents had already moved to Palestine, and they were the ones—together with my parents—who wanted to match up Karla and me in Israel after the war. That was a pretty absurd idea from a physical perspective, but I liked her because she radiated something lovable and uncomplicated.

We had something in common. She was among the *chaverim* who were in direct contact by letter with the Swiss Hechalutz office. That meant not so much "reports to the head office" as simply a connection to the outside world. Nathan Schwalb was situated in Geneva, and he coordinated the information exchange between the legal and illegal Jewish institutions and groups all over.

Originally, the world Hechalutz center concentrated on *aliyah* preparation and organizing emigration and immigration. After the beginning of the war, however, with the growing persecution of Jews by the Nazis in all countries they either occupied or were allied with, these tasks were joined by the establishment of a Relief and Rescue Committee. It was a complex network of contact people in the major cities and towns, in ghettos, kibbutzim, and later even in the concentration camps. It was also important to raise funds. Schwalb provided the German *chaverim* with information they would otherwise never have had access to and tried to warn them in time and encourage them to flee.

Karla was one of the many recipients of his letters. The developments in the summer and fall of 1941 made "Jewish addresses" increasingly risky. That's why they were looking for unsuspicious addresses. I don't remember whether it was Lotte or Karla who suggested my Christian mother as an address. In any case, from then on we would receive letters from Switzerland addressed to Frau Hedwig Beck. Inside they would then say, "Dear Alfred (Selbiger)" or "Dear Lotte," but everything was worded to sound like harmless family letters and stories. Delicate terms would be written in Hebrew, which evidently didn't serve to rouse the suspicions of the mail censors. If anyone at all had understood the language, everything would have been discovered very quickly. This connection to the outside world and the state of affairs regarding Zionism was absolutely essential for psychological and emotional survival. Even if our own *aliyah* seemed to be fading further and further from our grasp, we were able to maintain a consciousness that the struggle for Eretz Israel was continuing.

4

T HE FIRST TRANSPORT in late September 1941 was followed by many more. The "migration," carried out by the Gestapo and Jewish forced helpers, progressed in a thoroughly organized and structured manner. It had a certain Prussian correctness, almost a legitimacy. On the one hand, the victims had been worn down through years of oppression; on the other hand, they tried to face even this new hardship with dignity and pride. "No one should be able to say anything bad about us." And "We'll show those Germans just what Jews are made of!"

Street by street, people were told to prepare for their departure. They received a letter with a detailed information sheet, lists of objects that could be taken with them, instructions how to leave their apartments. Those who were notified had to either report to the assembly camp themselves or else—always early in the morning—they would be picked up by truck by the Gestapo or Jewish marshals. The marshals helped, comforted, calmed. They were in charge of taking care of the intended deportees until one thousand people had been gathered; then the trains left. In the beginning old passenger trains were used; later it was freight or cattle cars. The terrible Nazi term "transport" was truly fitting.

As of October 26, 1941, every legal form of real emigration was prohibited for Jews. For us Zionist young people, the idea of making our own *aliyah* became a total illusion—though one we continued to hold on to tightly. We didn't have anything else. Farewells became commonplace. More and more acquaintances and friends would say they had received their lists. The first reaction was always to give them courage. Then you'd repress in your mind the question of if and when your turn would come.

Information about what really happened in the east didn't start trickling in until 1942. Rumors were heard on BBC radio about "abuse" during

60

the transports and in the concentration camps. Nathan warned us in a letter not to comply with the order to "migrate"; he knew already that the Nazis had begun systematically murdering the Jews.

Then I met a remarkable woman through Jizchak Schwersenz. She had decided she was going to save as many Jews as she possibly could from deportation. Her name was Edith Wolff; we called her Ewo.

Ewo was born in 1904 in Berlin. She too was a *mischling* from a family with a Christian mother and Jewish father. Although her parents had baptized her as a Protestant, she felt Jewish and in 1933, as an act of political protest, converted to Judaism. An aunt saw to it that her membership card vanished from the files of the Jewish Community in 1936, so she remained unchecked for the time being and could work all the better against the Nazis.

It began with little "pinpricks," as she later called them, such as making anti-Nazi remarks in public, marking library books that expounded Nazi propaganda, or sending anonymous mass postcards "to the German people"—for example, when wearing the yellow star was introduced—with the following text: "Deutschland is now called Braunschweig [i.e., the German city of Brunswick]: One half wears Nazi brown [*braun*] and the other half remains silent [*schweigt*]." Another action she (and others) took was systematically riding the Berlin S-Bahn without paying—to undermine the state.

Once Ewo started working together with Recha Freier, the "Mother of the Youth Aliyah," her illegal actions became more directed. I knew the Freiers, since I shared a bench with Recha's sons at the synagogue. They lived not far from us, near the Friedrichshain park.

Recha Freier had a falling-out with the Reich Association of Jews in 1940 when she tried to arrange forged emigration certificates for Polish Jews interned in the Sachsenhausen camp. Alfred Selbiger of the Youth Aid and Paul Eppstein from the Reich Association were both devoted Zionists. They saw her action as risking the options for legal emigration, possibly making things worse for the Jews. In the end, Recha Freier was suspended from her position with the Youth Aid. Ewo had to leave as well since she was the only coworker who had supported the idea. They were no longer allowed to set foot in the Palestine Office.

In 1942 Ewo was working as a clerk at the Diederich city directory publishers. She used her position there to help Jews living incognito or in hiding, and her boss covered for her. First came the helpers in her immediate circle—friends and employees of her parents. Soon she got to know a group of Christians who were prepared to do something to help persecuted Jews: Franz Kaufmann and Helene Jacobs of the German Confessional

Church; Protestant minister Heinrich Grüber; secondary school teacher Bertha Gerhardt; teacher Elisabeth Abegg, a Quaker; Gertrud Luckner of the Catholic Action; and Ernst Hallermann of the Paulus Bund, the League of St. Paul of Non-Aryan Christians. Together with them, Ewo organized lodging and food, money, and ways to emigrate illegally for some of the large number of Jews who had gone underground on their own once the deportations started. I was also able to count on these helpers later, with my own illegals.

Ewo was in love with Jizchak. This small, energetic woman with the dark, short hair and round glasses was hopelessly smitten by the good-looking teacher who, like her, continued his dangerous political activities as best he could. In early 1942 she started pressuring him to save himself and go underground. Jizchak couldn't imagine leading a double life, hiding like a coward with false papers—after all, he was a Prussian-raised Jew! Amazingly, Ewo never managed to decide to live illegally either; the mere notion of constantly having to give the Nazi salute everywhere brought on feelings of nausea in her. But she believed that a Zionist Jew especially had to save himself for Eretz Israel instead of "letting himself be slaughtered like an animal by the Nazis."

In the Youth Aid and the German Hechalutz, the opposite opinion prevailed. Alfred Selbiger believed the Hechalutz pioneers had the "holy obligation" to lead the Jews, even to deportation. After a heated debate— it was sometime in early summer; I wasn't part of the youth leadership and hadn't attended the meetings—the political direction was decided: If the fate of our people takes them to the east, if that is what happens, then we shall go with our families on the transports, staying with the elderly, the sick, the weak.

Alfred Selbiger was a symbol of integration in Jewish youth work. Despite a somewhat melancholy aura, he was a warmhearted and impressive man filled with an iron sense of responsibility. In the summer of 1939 he had attended the Zionist congress in Switzerland—and then returned to Germany! For himself, he never considered emigration. "Everyone is replaceable," he once said, "but we need everyone!" His response to the deportations was "We are living history, and we must live up to it!" Fate could not bend him, only break him.

In August 1942 we received a letter from Nathan Schwalb in Geneva. It resparked the debate. He warned us again about the death camps in Eastern Europe and told the Berlin Hechalutz leadership to do everything in its power to help as many Jews as possible avoid deportation, either by fleeing or going underground.

By then I was allowed to open Nathan's letters. They already trusted me that much even though I wasn't part of the youth leadership. I took the letter to Lotte Kaiser as fast as I could. I was surprised by her reaction. With a thoughtful look, she asked, "Do you think we could hide my Aaron in Berlin?" Her love made her want to save her friend from the deportations rather than simply follow "orders from above."

It was also in August that Jizchak got his lists. The moment had come. What would he decide? Ewo was away at the time with her mother, but he had promised to telegraph her immediately. He did, and then he went to Selbiger. He didn't want to do anything without Selbiger's approval. It was his way of seeking a substitute legitimacy, as it were, for his step into illegality.

At first Alfred insisted that the Hechalutz could not suggest living underground, especially not to the younger *chaverim,* in order not to tear families apart. But then he made a surprising exception for Jizchak: "Okay, you give it a try, and then we'll talk about it again."

Jizchak Schwersenz was the first important person in the Hechalutz who faced deportation. His family had already been separated. His mother had been deported the past February; his father had been held back at first but picked up a little later. So Selbiger modified the "permission" to enter an illegal existence, making it into a mission. Schwersenz was to survive in order to "bear witness" for posterity of the work of the German Hechalutz and the Youth Aliyah. He even got one hundred marks a month from the unofficial till of the Hechalutz; the transfer was to be made conspiratorially at Alexanderplatz.

I think it was the same for Jizchak as it was for Ewo, and Lotte, and later for me too. In the end, love was the final factor in making the decision to live illegally. If he stayed in Berlin, he could be around his boys. So he took the step toward becoming incognito. After giving up his apartment and leaving a few belongings to "take-cAryans," Jizchak went to the Grunewald forest. He went in wearing the yellow star. He came out wearing a pin of the German Labor Front. Ewo had procured it, along with identity papers for his double existence. No less a person than Ernst Hallermann of the Paulus League had offered his passport. Among Ewo's illegal Jews there was a graphic artist, Günther Rogoff, who arranged the forged papers, putting Jizchak's picture in Hallermann's passport. Jizchak went to live with Ewo in the apartment she shared with her mother in the Friedenau district. The "test case" had everything he needed.

In the summer of 1942 I started thinking more and more seriously about going underground myself. I knew I didn't want to go to any "work camp" in Poland. What would be the sense in that? I knew that things were not better for the Jews in Poland than they were in Berlin. I couldn't speak any Polish, and the work would certainly not be easier than here.

Acquaintances of ours had received postcards from Lodz (called Litzmannstadt under the Nazis). Families who had been deported reported that they now lived in the former ghetto in apartments bigger than the ones they had in Berlin—only dirtier and messy! They still hadn't been given work, but "don't worry," etc., etc.

That seemed really strange to me. Didn't anyone wonder what had happened to the Jews who used to live in those apartments? Where had they "emigrated" to?

I didn't even have an inkling of the mass murder that had already begun. I simply didn't want to leave, and I didn't want to lose my family and my closest friends. In my city I could count on a network of people I trusted, Jews and Christians alike; I knew the ropes here. Illegality was my—our—only chance of surviving together.

In a conversation with Uncle Wobbi, my first secret lodgings were decided upon. In his house in Teltow, there was that basement storage room directly accessible from the garage that he had once offered me in case of emergency. Since Miriam and I were *mischlings* and doing forced labor in the armaments industry, we were not among those being deported, but we didn't feel very safe even so. Manfred and his whole family, as *Volljuden*, "full Jews," would inevitably get their lists, sooner or later.

During one of our air raid patrols, I brought up the unpleasant subject. Both of us were afraid, as it became more and more clear how our world was going up in flames. We embraced and tried to give each other some strength. With all the exuberance of youthful love we swore that nothing would separate us even though everything was getting out of control. I was happy to tell him about the hiding place at Uncle Wobbi's.

Among our friends, there were about eight or nine others who also wanted to go underground, including Karla Wagenberg. It was my first *mifkad,* if you will, like a patrol in scouting. Because of the deportations, many groups started breaking up. Our radius of movement was small, and our meetings took place more and more by coincidence. For that reason also, the idea of living illegally seemed to make such sense to me. Once you gave up your official existence as a Jew, you could move around the city and meet each other more freely.

I tried to talk as many friends as possible into making the move before they got their lists. But when it came down to it, they all decided in the same way: I can't leave my mother alone! There were lots of tearful scenes. I got some surprising farewell letters from a few girls that sounded almost like love letters: It's you I desired; my last letter is my first kiss. Sometimes

I visited friends on the day before they were picked up. I once spent the whole night playing chess with one fellow, and in the morning the Gestapo was at the door. I showed my identity card and was allowed to go—because my name wasn't on the list. They could have simply taken me with them—how could I have shown any resistance? But they didn't. Germans are Germans.

In October 1942 I was transferred overnight to the so-called potato operation at the Stettiner train station. The two years I had worked at EPeKo came to an abrupt end, but the friendships I made there continued. I never lost contact with Mamsi, but it was more difficult with Erwin. Shortly after I was transferred, he sabotaged the factory. A homemade bomb exploded and damaged the factory to such an extent that parts of it had to be closed. Erwin wasn't caught, but he was deported in 1943. He was sent to Auschwitz—and survived.

My new job was vitally necessary for the city. The Berlin population had to be supplied with enough potatoes for the coming winter. They were brought in from outside the city, and forced workers did the loading and unloading. Since some sackfuls were rotten, it reeked to high heaven when the cars were opened. At first the trains arrived every hour, but that couldn't be maintained because of the air raids. Then the boss would send us home. "We have to wait seven hours for the next train. Go home and come back this evening." If I organized things well, that would open up an incredible amount of flexibility for me. Whenever I got a chance to leave, I could get together with friends who didn't have to work until the afternoon or evening.

Since I was constantly on the move, I didn't see much of my family. The Christian relatives heard all about what I was doing through my mother, and they were worried: "That boy really has guts, but he's got to be careful!" Then Erich and Edith Nehlhans moved in with some Romanian friends they had met through the synagogue, which meant we had to vacate the apartment. We ended up moving in with the Rosenthals, one floor higher.

My sister and Günther, the youngest son, fell in love. Miriam came home from work at Siemens stinking indescribably of oil—if you ask me, she still smelled like that after the war. She always wanted to take a bath immediately and scrub herself thoroughly. My mother always wondered what took so long. Once she sat down in the kitchen—the bathroom was right through the door—in order to look into the matter inconspicuously. At some point the water stopped running, the door opened, and around the corner tiptoed my sister and the Rosenthal boy! They had their fun every day in the bathtub. My mother wasn't very happy about it, but not because it shocked her. She had other things to worry about.

Although everyone turned a blind eye to whatever we boys were up to with each other, relationships between boys and girls were treated much more seriously. It was the classical first step to forming a family and thus had predictably unpredictable consequences. In addition, everyone knew marriage affected one's place on the Nazi scale of discrimination. Whereas two *Volljuden*, or "full Jews," made their lives more difficult through marriage, two *mischlings*, from "mixed" marriages, would have been considered more "Aryan," so to speak. If Manfred had showed up with a Jewish girlfriend, his parents certainly would have intervened. But they didn't worry about his youthful escapades with me. A relationship between Miriam and the "full Jew" Rosenthal could do nothing but make things more difficult for her as a *mischling*.

This distinction gradually became ingrained into our consciousness through our everyday experiences. For example, my mother had to stand in line twice for food ration cards, once for her "German" one and once for our "Jewish" ones. There she would meet other women living in "mixed" marriages. They would exchange news and opinions and worries. "My daughter is working at the Jewish cemetery," said one woman. "I don't know if that's such a good idea, to be just with Jews. She'd be better off around other *mischlings*, for the future. . . ." Even though we felt like Jews, for everyday survival our thoughts were more pragmatic. And the Christian relatives seemed like security for us. Even today, the term *mischling* sometimes turns up in political debate. Heinz Galinski, who was the head of the Berlin Jewish Community until his death in 1992, always insisted, "Stop talking of *mischlings!* That's a Nazi word!" And that's exactly why we couldn't ignore it back then.

The Rosenthals considered themselves relatively safe since the father's first wife had been a Christian, and they'd even had a child. But that turned out not to be the case. They were deported to Theresienstadt. Even though this camp had a "good reputation"—it was considered less severe, more like a ghetto than a concentration camp—my sister was of course desperately unhappy. She wanted to fling herself down the stairs when the Gestapo came to pick up her first big love.

Aaron Menczer was also deported to Theresienstadt, in October 1942, together with his whole Viennese group. Lotte was absolutely devastated. The next disaster followed quickly. In November the Reich Association officially announced the death of Alfred Selbiger and seven other members who had been arrested along with him.

Their murder was like a gruesome echo of what had happened in late

May. After the Baum resistance group bombed the Nazi exhibition cyni-
cally entitled "The Soviet Paradise," all leading members of the Reich Association, including the elderly rabbi Leo Baeck and Alfred Selbiger, were
taken hostage by the Gestapo. After waiting for hours with their faces to
the wall, they were told that to "atone" for the crime, 250 Jews would be
selected at random and shot.

And now, once again, the Reich Association was being made responsible for all forms of sabotage done by Jews. Twenty people did not report
to the assembly camp when they were supposed to. That was called sabotage, and twenty representatives of the Reich Association were arrested;
eight of them were executed.

The funeral service for the dead took place in our apartment. Sonja
Okun took over Alfred Selbiger's position; Lotte gave the eulogy. She was
shocked and bitter; I hardly recognized her. "We have betrayed Alfred,"
she said. "All of us who spoke out in favor of becoming illegal have driven
him and the others to their deaths." She meant me too. I don't think she
could distinguish anymore between her despair at Aaron's being unable to
take on an illegal existence and her outrage over the murder of Alfred and
the others, which really did seem like the price that was paid for the twenty
who had gone underground.

Aaron never would have left his group anyway. Maybe she knew that.
Only a short time later, Lotte was picked up. She too was brought to
Theresienstadt. I am certain that she went standing tall—without "betray-
ing" her Aaron. Neither of them survived.

It got increasingly quiet around those of us who were still left. And then it
happened. Even when you expect a catastrophe, it always comes too soon.
The Lewins got their lists. Just a few months before, they had repainted
their apartment, probably painted right over the bugs; in any case it had
badly needed a new coat. And now they were supposed to leave. When I
heard the news, I wanted to see Manfred right away to arrange how he
could get to Uncle Wobbi. But communication between us had gotten more
difficult around that time, as I had just started checking out how much leeway I had at the potato job.

A few days later I spoke with Manfred's younger brother Rudi, who
worked nights and had come to the early morning meeting of the remnants
of our group right after his shift that day. He said to me, "Can you come
by this evening? Manfred will be there." That was my chance. No new
potato shipment was supposed to arrive that day.

When I got to Dragonerstrasse that evening, only Rudi and Schlomo
were there. The rest of the Lewin family had been picked up early in the

morning by the marshals. The night shift had spared the two brothers sitting before me from being taken as well. The two of them sat in the empty apartment, absolutely determined to report to the predeportation assembly camp on Grosse Hamburger Strasse the next morning. The camp had been set up in October 1942 to supplement the one on Levetzowstrasse, later replacing it entirely.

The Lewins had surely thought about their situation—at the very latest, once they received their lists. They didn't expect to be sent to an extermination camp. The mother, the youngest son, who suffered from asthma, the hunchbacked Rudi, and the little girl: All of them counted on the father—after all, there's always a demand for barbers, isn't there—and on the two strong sons, Manfred and Schlomo. The motto of the youth leadership had always been "We're staying together!" And the same certainly applied for the Lewins. For me, in love and selfish as I was, this sentence had a different meaning—I did not want to be separated from Manfred.

The atmosphere within the Lewins' four empty walls was strangely mixed. I was in absolute despair, almost panic-stricken. The brothers were sad and anything but confident, though at the same time they were composed and determined to hold on to the only certainty they had left: They would see their family the next day, and together they would face the events to come.

It was one of many goodbyes, and for me it was without a doubt the hardest of all. They were my last connection to Manfred, and even that would be lost all too soon. I screamed and cried, and they couldn't calm me down. I hardly even registered that they were there until Schlomo took me in his arms to comfort me. He started to cry too.

What happened then was not all that surprising; we made love. Maybe he had been envious at times of the happy moments Manfred had spent with me. Now he was facing an uncertain fate, and this was perhaps his last chance to experience closeness, unguarded and without danger. For me it was like a farewell from Manfred, a goodbye I never had the chance to say. Little Rudi snuggled up to us and sobbed. I don't know what he thought about the situation, if he understood it at all. The tragedy and the graveness of the moment aroused a desperate passion in Schlomo and me.

Early the next morning the two of them, unwavering, made their way to Grosse Hamburger Strasse. Everything was spinning around in my head; I was feverishly thinking of some way to save Manfred. Finally I thought I could try his boss, Lothar Hermann the painter. The authorities thought well of him, yet Manfred had told me he was a friendly man, typical Berlin working class, a small businessman, gruff but warmhearted, with a direct and rather uncomplicated disposition. I went to him without knowing exactly what I had in mind.

The business was located in an apartment on Gipsstrasse that had been refurbished to accommodate the paint and materials warehouse and a small office. It was still dark outside, but the teams of painters were already off to work. As I stood in front of Hermann, I took a deep breath and said, "I'm here to excuse Manfred Lewin. He was picked up yesterday." The man was moved, but not all that much. It wasn't anything new for him to "lose" workers in this way. "I would like to try to get him out," I said, cautiously groping for the right words. I thought maybe he would give me a letter saying that Manfred was indispensable or something like that. "Yeah, Manfred is a good boy," Hermann responded jovially, and I could see his mind clicking away.

"I have an idea," he said, scrutinizing me, "if you have the nerve." His eyes lit up. What did he mean? My mind was a blank; we could have waited forever for me to come up with any ideas. "I'll do anything," I answered.

"My son just went to work," he said. "His Hitler Youth uniform is hanging over there. It would fit you for sure; he's about as big as you. If you show up wearing it. . . ."

Risky, but ingenious. I put on the uniform. It was at least four sizes too big, and the way it hung from my shoulders made me look like a scarecrow. As makeshift alterations I tucked the sleeves and legs up on the inside, hoping that it wouldn't be conspicuous. If I had been in the SS, I would've arrested someone looking like me on the spot. I couldn't have looked more suspicious.

It wasn't far to Grosse Hamburger Strasse. I shuffled along cautiously so the pant legs wouldn't slip down, and I tried out several variations of the story I was about to tell. The assembly camp was set up in two adjacent buildings, the former Jewish Old Age Home and my old school. As I walked through the entrance gate I calmed down completely. It wasn't a threatening place for me. One of the Jewish marshals stationed outside eyed me skeptically. Did he know me? Things were constantly going on there that weren't totally kosher. People kept coming up and wanting to know, Is my brother-in-law inside, Are the you-know-whos already gone, Could you take a note inside. . . . There was a lot of bribery, and the marshals often turned a blind eye to little things. But I was there as a Hitler Youth, and they didn't talk to Jewish marshals.

"Heil Hitler!" Not too abrupt; don't forget the sleeves. I marched inside. I said to the officer, "I would like to speak with the Obersturmbann-führer, please." At least I knew the rank, even though I didn't know the name. The Obersturmbannführer came right away. The whole thing was amazingly smooth and businesslike. The assembly camp, why it was there, what happened inside—none of that was of any particular interest to this man, although people's fates were decided there every day. Normal procedure in carrying out a policy that had been in effect for a year already: Jews were evacuated to be sent to labor service, one after another. Everyone went along with it. No big deal.

And now a little Hitler Youth—I was nineteen at the time and small anyway—was standing there asking about one of the Jews that had been picked up. "The Jew Manfred Israel Lewin was brought here yesterday. He worked for us and is a saboteur! He has the keys to several of the apartments we are renovating. Materials have also been stored there. My father sent me to get him so we can get back to work!" Luckily, Herr Obersturmbannführer didn't ask any questions; of course Manfred didn't have any keys.

They got Manfred. When he saw me, his eyes twitched. I covered up any awkwardness by quickly saying, "You kept the keys! Now come with me and tell us exactly which key goes to which apartment, so we can get back to work!" My voice was calm, but sharp and clear. One sentence was pounding inside me: Get out of here fast; just get out of here with him fast!

The SS man had already started turning away. The case was closed for him. "But you'll bring him right back?!" he added. "What would I want with a Jew?" I answered. In this situation, at that time, a man like that was thinking neither of illegal Jews nor of the "final solution." The entire incident was not especially interesting to him. He laughed, and we left.

I walked out of my old school building onto the street. The buildings were familiar, the sidewalk, the streetlamps. I was back in my world, with my Manfred next to me. I was filled with a combination of triumph and security as we walked down the street together, past the former Old Age Home, past the entrance to the cemetery, with its couple of trees. Only a few minutes. I beamed at him, held out a twenty-mark bill—quite a bit for those times—and said quietly, "Here's some money. Now go to my uncle in Teltow like we discussed and wait for me. I'll come as soon as I can."

He stood there, took the twenty marks, and looked at me. "Gad, I can't go with you. My family needs me. If I abandon them now, I could never be free." No smile, no sadness. He had made his decision. We didn't even say goodbye. He turned around and went back.

In those seconds, watching him go, I grew up.

I NEVER SAW MANFRED AGAIN. And I never really got over the loss. Years later, his name still electrified me—even in the Hebrew form, Meir. I literally chased after men named Manfred, since I had lost mine, my Manfred. Perhaps that was an immature way to mourn, but it was all I had, aside from repressing the pain and distracting myself. I buried myself in activities, since I didn't want to lose any more of my few remaining friends. I hid some of them for short periods of time. And of course there was the mindless job at the Stettiner station.

Our "potato group" was comprised almost entirely of *mischlings*, and then there was a group of Italian antifascists that had been brought to Germany to do slave labor. Imagine a huge, ugly, partially bombed-out train station, drafty, dim, and dirty. Unloading the potato sacks was actually quite pleasant. The foremen were all Germans, elderly gentlemen who didn't have to serve in the military. They didn't push us all that much, and if you bribed them with a few cigarettes they were almost friendly.

We spent our meal breaks in a protected corner on the train platform. One of the younger, more handsome Italian boys caught my attention, since he spoke some broken German. His name was Giovanni, and I picked him out . . . to be my distraction.

For an Italian he was unusually tall and thin, with black curly hair, fiery eyes, and soft lips that turned up at the corners happily. Even back then that was an important detail for me. I keep away from people with turned-down mouths. Much too much trouble to get them turned up. In other words, he appealed to me.

First of all, I made an effort to work on the same cars as he did, and then I started to beguile him. It worked amazingly well. He saw how I was struggling with the heavy, dirty sacks—of course I made sure to suffer all the more when he was around—and soon he was standing near me and helping the little guy with the heavy shipment.

But how could I be any more obvious, with all the monitoring and observation? I didn't know of any helpful guidebooks with tips for such a situation: How do you pick up a foreign prisoner while doing slave labor unloading potato sacks? I resorted to pretty primitive means; the simplest is often the best. Winter came, and it got colder and colder. I forgot my gloves a few times. It was obvious that at some point I simply wouldn't be able to work anymore. He noticed that too. Since we stood rather close together when heaving the sacks back onto the cars, no one noticed his solution to my problem. He took one of my hands and—to warm it up—placed it in the pocket of his pants. In there things were really pretty hot. . . .

We hugged each other briefly, nothing more. One or two days later he said to me, "We could get together if you want. I can take you back with me to our camp." They were housed in a converted schoolhouse on Prenzlauer Allee. So I visited him there. He even had some Italian red wine, which was totally new for me.

I ended up sleeping there often. He was just bringing a coworker home with him. Since we had to get up and out very early in the morning, I simply stayed over. In his bed, in a dormitory room with sixty men—that was the most normal thing in the world. I still enjoy reminiscing about Giovanni's curly hair.

It was more reasonable to sleep over somewhere than to come home late. After all, there was an eight o'clock curfew for Jews (nine o'clock in the summer). Every house had its troublemaker, a block leader or informer, who watched to make sure the Jews got home on time.

At Prenzlauer Strasse 12a, Heinz Blümel was the resident pest. When we moved in, in 1938, Frau Szczepanski warned us: "The Blümels from the side building are staunch Nazis. On top of that, they hate Jews because they always wanted to move into the front building [with apartments facing the street instead of the courtyard], but those apartments are always filled with Jews. So be careful!" And the Blümels were indeed malicious, especially their son Heinz. He had a hump on his back that was so big you could've sat on if it had been cut off—another hunchback in my life.

But he wasn't a typical hunchback; he was relatively tall and good-looking. He had a definite neck and didn't look deformed at all. He simply had this monstrosity on his shoulder. Heinz Blümel always ran around in his uniform. I don't know if he was in the SA or if they still let him be in the Hitler Youth, even though he was already twenty. In any case, he marched around constantly and clearly as a Nazi.

After 1941 Jews were not allowed to use the same air raid shelters as "Aryans." Kneifel, the successor to the old baker Schulz, rest his soul, immediately said, "Jews are welcome to come to me in the bakery. Next to my oven it's just as safe." Blümel father and son were outraged: Jews were absolutely prohibited from entering buildings where food for Germans was produced. As air raid wardens, their word was final. So we had to go into the front corner of the basement, which was more like a semiunderground room, with barred windows to the street. If a bomb had fallen in the street we would've been finished.

Heinz took up a position almost every evening at the entrance to the building to control movements in and out. If I came back late, which due to my activities was not seldom the case, he would yell and throw me contemptuous looks. Without question he would report me for it someday. I wonder why he didn't do it right away.

One evening—it was early 1943—something unexpected happened. As always, I was running late; the sirens were sounding, and I was greeted at the door by the Blümel boy. "Come on, get in quick," he blurted at me. "The planes are already approaching." And he pushed me toward the cellar. My parents were already there; my sister was at Siemens. There was something different in his voice; what was with him? Suddenly I noticed that he wasn't wearing a uniform. . . . Strange.

The bombardment had barely finished when he came over to our corner of the basement and said to me, "Hey, you! Come with me, we're going to do the rounds! We have to check if the roof is okay. Some bombs dropped near our building, and it might have been damaged too." I was still surprised. The attic had been made generally accessible. The shedlike compartments that used to be assigned to individual tenants had been removed because of the fire hazard. We stood in the large open space where, obviously, nothing had happened. Somewhat uncertain, I walked around as though I wanted to check it out more closely.

All of a sudden, the boy turned to me, tears streaming down his face. He came over to me and pushed me against the wall. "Do you know what they did to me?" he sobbed. "I'm not allowed to wear a uniform anymore because of my hump!"

To be honest, it was not difficult to believe that the Nazis did not want to have someone with a huge hump on his shoulder serving as a shining example of "Aryan" masculinity by wearing a uniform. I really felt sorry for him. "I have devoted my whole life to them! And now they throw me out!" He got more and more angry, then started screaming.

I had to quiet him. Any kind of fuss was bad. Since he no longer seemed so dangerous, I dared to walk over to him. I had lost my fear; he seemed to have channeled his rage toward the Nazis, who had ostracized him. I laid my hand on his arm to calm him. He looked at me, hurt and angry.

"Forget about it, it's not the end of the world." Nothing better came to my mind. "There are other ways to make something of your life."

He threw me an almost pleading glance. "Can I work with you all?" At first I didn't understand him; it sounded too absurd. "I know that friends of yours sleep up here. That you hide people up here!" I felt nauseous from the shock. He could have long since denounced us! A few boys had slept here a few times and stupidly enough had forgotten to put their blankets away. Frau Szczepanski had also noticed. And now he wanted to work with us?

We were still standing pretty close together. My mind was clicking away, trying to figure out whether I could believe and trust him. That picture of misery could still be a potential risk. Then he came closer, and I felt something firm and bulging between his legs. That was the very last thing I would have expected! Instead of stepping away, he pressed his body closer against mine, hardly noticeably, as though he were cautiously suggesting something. I murmured, "Oh, let's talk about it later." With that, I meant both of his "requests."

A few days later he did something clever. He had heard about my nightly air raid patrols, and now he registered as well. "I signed us both up," he announced. "I'm still allowed to do air raid patrols." Ever since my nights of love with Manfred I had avoided the place. Meanwhile there was almost no one left with whom I could have gone on patrol. So now I was going with Heinz Blümel. As eerie as it sounds, that's where it happened. He knew what he wanted, and I let him do it, half numb from the sadness.

From that day on, we spoke very openly with each other. "Don't say a word to my parents," he warned. Now *he* was the one who meant both, our affair and his offer of help. "What can I do for you?" He rented a nearby basement apartment and gave me the spare key so I could let people sleep there. I didn't do it very often because the entrance could be observed from everywhere on the street. That was too risky for me.

Despite his hump he could ride a bicycle, and I used him as a messenger throughout most of the war. No one checked the papers of a hunchback! Especially not a notorious Nazi like him. He ended up transporting all kinds of food and other things for us. . . .

I don't know what became of Heinz Blümel. He survived the war, but I lost touch with him at some point and was unable to locate him again.

ONE EVENING ALL THE FORCED WORKERS at the train station (except the Italians, of course) were handed a piece of paper saying we had to report to the Employment Office for Jews the next day because the potato job was coming to an end. I got all dressed up the next morning—knee-length pants and boots; I looked very sporty and smart, and off I went.

At the entrance I thought, Strange, it's really crowded here, so many trucks parked in front. . . . When it was my turn, I handed my notice to the man at the desk, and he looked in the files. "Yeah, yeah," he said, "go over to the truck on the left. There's a new job for you; they'll take you there." There were four other workers on the truck already, and we quickly figured out what we had in common—we were all *mischlings*. I expected a rather harmless position, since there were also older men on our truck. We had to wait for hours, and more and more workers joined us before the truck finally took off.

That was February 27, 1943, the day of the so-called Factory Operation, at the end of which Goebbels wanted to announce that Berlin was *judenrein*, purged of Jews. It was to be his present to Adolf Hitler for his fifty-fourth birthday in April. All the Jews and *mischlings* still in Berlin were registered with the employment office. He simply ordered them all to report there, and most of them did, I among them. The big armaments factories such as Siemens and Telefunken needed their workers and retained them despite this order. Goebbels then had the workers removed from the factories, sometimes even using military force. After all, Hitler had already ordered in September 1942 that Jews be gradually removed from the armaments industry, irrespective of the objections from economic experts that the skilled Jewish workers were indispensable. Now not only the armaments industry but the entire city was to be made *judenrein*. In March there were still 27,250 Jews living in the city; in April there were 18,300; in June the number had been reduced to 6,800. On June 19, 1943, Goebbels triumphantly—though falsely—announced that the goal had been reached.

The former administrative building of the Jewish Community at Rosenstrasse 2–4 was one of the buildings converted to an internment camp during the Factory Operation. This is where those "related to Aryans" were held. On the way there I experienced one of the most dreadful, disheartening moments of my life. Now I was in their hands! But as soon as I was in the building all my fears fell by the wayside. Well, I thought, if I can't change the fact that I am here now, at least maybe I could find Manfred. I also thought of the other trucks. They were obviously still making some kind of distinctions, or else they would have deported us all together. I started feeling almost calm.

The building on Rosenstrasse consisted of large, sometimes huge, empty offices and conference rooms, in which the people they brought here by the truckload had to camp. A small number of offices were occupied by SS people and their secretaries.

Right at the entrance one of the Jewish marshals, whom I had gone to school with, recognized and greeted me cheerfully. In those first few hours questions, rumors, and opinions were buzzing back and forth, and the marshals tried to calm everyone down. We were evidently not about to face the worst—that is, immediate deportation.

The place was filled with men only—fathers, sons, older men—who were crying: What will my mother say, or my (Christian) wife? Initially, I was told to stay in my room; I was a prisoner like everyone else. I looked around and saw a boy who immediately appealed to me. He smiled at me somewhat coyly, and I answered his message without words. His father, sitting next to him, was very reserved and didn't smile.

I stayed near him, and finally we started talking to each other. The boy told me about the last trip he had taken with his father, to the Tessin area in southern Switzerland, and how beautiful it had been there. In passing he mentioned that his father had worked in the Hermann Göring factory. "Nothing will happen to us. My father has connections." The next day the father was picked up in a Mercedes. He was a scientist named Israel and belonged to the so-called Göring Jews. A little while later the boy was also released. It felt good to spend that first night in the camp with the boy—stolen displays of affection in the dark, spooned against his back. And I thought to myself, If such privileged people are here too, things can't get all that bad.

The next morning we were ordered into the courtyard in groups. An SS man asked questions. "Is there a good jazz pianist here?" A few raised their hands and were selected out. Then, "Is there a specialist in horse breeding?" And so on. Six or seven professions were called out. Whoever raised their hands left the camp. The marshal I knew seemed relieved to find me still there. "Don't volunteer for anything!" he whispered to me. The specialists were all taken to Auschwitz.

Around noon of the first day something happened that often still works today. If I am feeling good, I seem to inspire people's confidence. An Austrian SS man everyone was afraid of inspected the rooms, saw me, and called out, "The little guy there, he can do the control rounds!" My boots and breeches definitely did the trick. I was given an armband and went from room to room. If anyone had any special needs or wishes, any emergencies, if there was anything important to report, then I would go into the office and relate the news. I could move around the whole building freely—and so I found my father and, that afternoon, in one of the rooms for women, my sister as well.

Miriam had narrowly escaped a catastrophe. She was picked up from work at Siemens, together with Edith Nehlhans. From there, the workers were all taken to a barracks; no distinctions were made. Edith realized very quickly what was going on, and she kept telling Miriam to go to the head SS man and say that she was only half Jewish. That was her only chance. He sent her back saying it didn't matter, she was wearing a star, wasn't she? She tried again. The second time she claimed her father worked for the Jewish Community. He said that wasn't true and didn't make a difference anyway, so she returned to the others. Edith wouldn't let up, so Miriam tried a third time. By that time he recognized her and remembered her name. Maybe he had checked it out in the meantime; in any case he said, "Okay, we'll send you to Rosenstrasse. But if we find out that you lied, you're ready for Siberia, got it?"

So she ended up in the building on Rosenstrasse too. Edith, who didn't have *mischling* status to take advantage of, couldn't avoid the transport to Auschwitz. It was Edith's stubbornness that saved Miriam's life; Miriam wouldn't have had the nerve if Edith hadn't been there. When she told me the story, I was terribly torn between a feeling of relief that Miriam and I were there, together; and mourning, that we had now lost Edith too; and anxiety about the recent worsening of our situation as a whole.

The atmosphere that evening was stifling. People slept restlessly; some cried. Little by little a feeling of horror spread. It's getting dangerous here, I kept thinking, until I finally remembered: If they wanted to send us on a transport, they wouldn't need to spend the time making all these distinctions—everyone at once and all together; that would be much easier!

The next morning the marshals were called together and sent to the entrance of the building. "Your relatives have thrown food packages on the doorstep. Distribute them!" That wasn't really necessary since we were fed there, and not badly, I must add. I took it as a good sign that they cooked for us. And then I saw my mother standing at the entrance.

The most important thing was not that I saw her but that she saw me — her son! Her son, who was allowed to wave to her. She could see how I picked up the packages and carried them inside. It must have been an incredible relief for her to see that I had been given a job to do. And at the moment I saw her, I realized that we were really still in the middle of Berlin, a few steps from the Hackescher Markt, and we were not in a death camp somewhere in the east.

On the third morning and every day after that, my aunts were there too; even my uncles came. Paul Krüger was there, and Willi, on leave from the front, marched up in full uniform. That was a real show of courage, the courage to stand up for one's beliefs. More and more people came and stood there, demonstrating against the regime. What an inner strength these *goyim* had developed! I always try to remember what it was like as they stood there in the middle of the city shouting, "Give us back our children! Give us back our husbands and wives!" Many of them had been totally apolitical citizens up to then. So that too was a show of German resistance, not just the officers involved in the July 20 plot to overthrow Hitler!

It gave me courage. After my young friend and his father had been released, I looked around for someone else I liked. My eye caught a really tall guy! I always managed to get close to him at night. When the lights were turned off, easily, effortlessly, we slid closer together. With so many people in one room the nights were anything but quiet anyway. In these huge halls, one would start moaning, another crying. Who was interested in checking out what was going on in the dark?

At that time I refined my method of making love when there are other people sleeping in the same room. No one should notice, but satisfaction should be possible nevertheless. Affection, gentleness, and letting go are the key words — it isn't always necessary to screw around until the walls shake! That also applied to the secret lodgings later on, where you weren't allowed to walk around, talk, or flush the toilets, so the neighbors wouldn't hear that people were living there. Where there's a will there's a way!

After the fourth day in the building on Rosenstrasse, I was certain we would be released. No one did anything to the demonstrators. And no transports were sent out, at least not from there. There was no more sign of the brutality that had been used in getting the workers out of the factories.

During the night of March 1, 1943, the British Royal Air Force flew a massive attack on Berlin. Bombers rumbled; antiaircraft units fired back; isolated bombardments could be heard. St. Hedwig's Hospital was hit. The all-clear signal didn't come until early the next morning.

A short time later, they were back in front of the building—the "women of Rosenstrasse," as they were later called, even though quite a few men were there too. According to later estimates, there were about a thousand people involved; about twice as many *mischlings* and Jews in "mixed" marriages had been interned inside.

It took until the end of the week before a decision was made. On March 4, in a surprise move, the SS set up machine guns aimed at the demonstrators. From inside all we could hear were the enraged screams of our relatives. "Unpleasant scenes" is how Goebbels referred to it in his diaries. Just as unexpectedly, the SS men cleared away the machine guns a few hours later. Not a shot had been fired.

Evidently the Nazis had decided that the Berlin population had been shocked enough from the most severe bombardments thus far in the war and that further cause for alarm should be avoided. On March 6—it was a Saturday—without much ado we were given our release certificates.

That was the end of our internment on Rosenstrasse. It was far more dangerous than we had been able to comprehend, but in the end this act of Goebbels had a paradoxical consequence. Since there were officially no more Jews in Berlin, we *mischlings* were safer than we were before. And for the "full Jews" the henchmen had missed, the only option still open to them was to be illegal.

There was a big, stocky man in the courtyard of Rosenstrasse 2–4 looking at us. His name was Richard Wählisch, and his company specialized in restoring bombed-out buildings and carting away rubble and debris. The more Berlin showed signs of the war, the more his business boomed. He could use some cheap workers like us, and we had just been released.

Wählisch walked through the rows, and then he said to the people he had selected, cheerfully yet rather awkwardly, since he seemed to have difficulty expressing himself, "You can all live at home, and you'll only work until the afternoon. You'll take care of the major damage. And I won't tolerate stealing. You start early tomorrow morning."

My father and I were on his new workforce. The girls and women who had been interned on Rosenstrasse, including Miriam, were put to work washing railroad cars at the Anhalter train station. You have to imagine these Germans—war was raging, but there was still an incredible amount of passenger travel, and the cars had to be clean, if you please. . . .

The joy at our family reunion at home was great, and soon Aunt Anna was at the door with a huge bouquet of roses. My mother, who had held herself together magnificently through the ordeal, was hit with blind rage. She ripped the roses out of Anna's hand and slapped her on the face. "Are you crazy to bring us roses?" "But Hedwig, what's the matter? It's a wonderful day, your husband and your children have been released. . . ." "And you bring us roses?! I'd rather have cigarettes or something to eat. Do you think we have too much to eat?" We were all speechless. She was yelling at her sister. It was difficult to understand, but my mother felt the pressure of knowing that things would not be much easier for us from then on. Her sisters, on the other hand, primarily felt the happiness and relief over our being set free, over the success of *their* act of resistance, and in such a situation you would buy flowers, wouldn't you!?

OUR FAMILY HAD SURVIVED Goebbels's Factory Operation. But what about our friends? I got in touch with Jizchak Schwersenz as quickly as possible.

Ewo and her mother were still hiding him. When I went there to visit, he was in high spirits. "On February 27 we founded the Chug Chaluzi." A new pioneer group. "You and Miriam are part of it, of course."

I was amused. It made sense to me that those still in Berlin get together in order to make plans according to the new situation. That we had to form a group called Chug Chaluzi was more in the direction of the scout structures that Jizchak loved. He had already prepared a program and seriously wanted to go on "field trips"! Of course the primary purpose was mutual support, especially with respect to the illegals, but he didn't want to abandon the familiar form of Zionist training he was so fond of—with all the trappings.

The group consisted of some of the recently released *mischlings* and some illegals. It grew quickly as others from my circle of friends joined in. In the beginning we were about fifteen. By summer the number had grown to thirty, including other friends with whom we kept in contact, in Berlin and in the work camps that had been set up at the former *hachsharot*.

Mamsi, whom I had kept in touch with ever since I'd been transferred from EPeKo, supported us from the very beginning, though of course she didn't take part in the Zionist training. By chance she had avoided being arrested and taken to Rosenstrasse. The notice telling her to report to the employment office wasn't delivered until March 5. When she appeared on March 6, she simply got a stamp on her papers and was sent away. Since she lived safely with her mother, she was a valuable helper for our newly founded group.

The significance of Jizchak's involvement at this point cannot be underestimated. He held us together and gave us the feeling that more was at stake than mere survival. But regarding practical needs for life in the underground—such as food, money, or false papers—he was not very talented. That was the task of Ewo and others.

The "workplan" for a week in the summer of 1943 has survived, serving as evidence of what Jizchak managed to organize despite his illegal status. Tuesday, eight to ten P.M., Hebrew and English lessons; Wednesday, six to nine P.M., meeting in Grunewald forest, where a historical paper was presented and instruction on Palestine was given; Thursday evening, practical questions pertaining to illegality were discussed; on the Sabbath, we were at the Littmanns' from three to nine P.M., reading and discussing *Hamlet* and listening to a talk on Solomon; on Sunday, we spent the whole day on an outing; and on Monday evening, the group went together to a Verdi and Schubert concert.

Even getting tickets for an event was a way for an illegal who had no lodgings to spend a night in relative safety. For some events, people got in line the evening before tickets went on sale, and the anonymity of the line provided protection until morning. Public events later turned into nasty traps, since the Gestapo started arranging the services of more and more Jewish *greifers,* or "snatchers." Most of them had lived illegally themselves and were now forced to help locate Jews in hiding. These people knew where illegals could be found.

Life got more dangerous, and there was less and less room for our group to operate. Jizchak's disguise was first-class. He had changed his appearance, wore a Nazi pin, and had the magnificently forged identity papers of Ernst Hallermann. But his scout games were risky for us as well. He would plan to meet his boys at the Westkreuz station, and there they were, a whole bunch of rather Jewish-looking boys standing around together to go on an outing. I found it dangerous, and it got on my nerves. But it cannot be denied that in this early phase we had Jizchak to thank for the inner cohesion of Chug Chaluzi.

One day in March 1943 two boys came to a meeting at our house. I knew one of them from Jizchak's previous group: Poldi Chones, a good-looking, impetuous fellow with an open, cheerful face. One of Jizchak's favorites, I remembered. The other one was Heinz Abrahamssohn, and I was seeing him for the first time. He was blond and had a quiet, mischievous smile and strangely deep, shaded eyes. A straightforward, masculine type. The two of them had managed to escape the Factory Operation by coincidence, but they had lost their families and had been struggling along on their own ever since. Initially I let them stay in our attic. I liked Heinz immediately, and we spent the entire night together talking.

At first Heinz was not at all interested in any kind of Zionist group. He had been part of the Jewish Sportgemeinschaft, the Athletics Association, which was a German-oriented club. His father had been on the board of the Reichsbund jüdischer Frontsoldaten, the Reich League of Jewish Front-Line Veterans from World War I, which also had almost nationalist leanings.

"On that day," he told me in his deep voice, "I finished work at six in the morning and went home without suspecting anything. Without a star on my jacket, by the way; I never wore it. I don't feel like it, and besides, I'm blond and have a small nose. . . ." I didn't necessarily agree; I thought he looked pretty Jewish, but I kept quiet. I liked him. "When I got home, my parents weren't there. But that's normal; we three usually had such different shifts that we practically only saw each other on the weekends. So I went to sleep until late afternoon and then went down to the street. All of a sudden I saw a column of trucks filled with SS people and police turn into Zehdenicker Strasse; that's where we lived. As I got closer, I could see that they were forcing people out of their houses and onto the trucks. I knew what was happening; they were making the rounds—big time."

His parents had been picked up directly from work at the factory. He had been lucky to have had the night shift. When the Gestapo arrived at the factory at seven in the morning, he had already gone home.

A Jewish Communist friend from work had once offered to help him if worst came to worst, and Heinz went to him immediately. He didn't live far away, in the Prenzlauer Berg district. But the man was suddenly too afraid to run away. The growing danger paralyzed him.

"I was furious and screamed at him. I couldn't believe that he would just let that happen to himself. Everyone saw it, how one family after another was picked up. I always just kept thinking: I don't want to get picked up! I don't want to leave! I don't want to leave! It was like a *dybbuk* in me. At least this guy gave me the address of a friend. I took off right away, and a little while later everyone was picked up from his street too."

Heinz didn't return to his parents' apartment until evening. It was still empty and abandoned. Outside there was a seal on the lock, but he opened it easily and went inside, where at least he found something to eat and drink. The next day he happened to run into Poldi, whom he knew from school, on the street. And now they were both sitting here with me, without a pfennig, without a family, without a place to stay.

They only stayed a few days, since it was impossible to keep it secret in the building. The second night the cot I put up in the attic for them collapsed underneath them, and my father heard it. When he went to check it out, he discovered the two of them. It was clear that they couldn't stay there for very long. But with Ewo's help they found another place to stay. They joined the Chug Chaluzi group, and from then on we saw each other regularly. That's when I found out that Heinz's Jewish middle name was Zwi. It was in his bar mitzvah book. So he didn't have to decide on a Hebrew version of his name like the rest of us. Meanwhile we all felt a certain sense of pride using our Hebrew names.

Jizchak didn't like Zwi very much. He noticed immediately that Zwi would not be part of the phalanx of "his boys." However, later they got to know each other better and became good friends, which they have remained to today.

Zwi's Jewish uncle Martin Grünberg had connections to someone working at the Reich Printing Office who printed double series of food ration cards. Zwi would meet a contact man at night at Alexanderplatz, buy a stack of cards, and make some money by selling them to Ewo, who helped illegals out with some of the problems of daily existence. That made the sixteen-year-old an indispensable man for us—and soon a target for the Gestapo.

I knew I had to take special care of him, since he had no one anymore, except for Uncle and Aunt Grünberg who lived in Blankenburg at the outskirts of the city. Soon we started seeing each other as often as we could.

It must have been obvious to him that I was also attracted to him physically, because things progressed with Zwi the same way they had with some others—that is, he made the first move, not me. We had gone to a lake in the Grunewald forest to go swimming, and we were lying in our swimming trunks under the trees. We were surprisingly relaxed even though bombers were flying overhead. It was an afternoon that seemed like part of a carefree childhood, I was thinking. Zwi was lying there quietly, deep in thought. Then at some point he embraced me; he was passionate, awkward, and at the same time tender. I was happy, but I held myself back, didn't push him. Our coming together was an incredibly slow process, cautious, and very loving. . . . We knew we could count on each other. Knowing that in the midst of the danger we were living every day brought out an overpowering feeling of attachment between us. From that fraternal trust, erotic feelings developed. That day in Grunewald Forest was the first time we made love.

Just as we finished, a man came up on a bicycle. He must have seen us, since he started whistling loudly as soon as he approached. Zwi laid down over me so we couldn't be seen all that clearly. We heard leaves and branches cracking on the forest path, and then the man was gone.

We laughed. "He must have thought I was a girl," I said to reassure Zwi. But that wasn't necessary. He didn't brood in hour-long conversations like Manfred.

Actually I knew right away that Zwi really needed a woman, despite all the passion. He, like others, sought the feminine in me. My dick didn't interest him much. But that is decisive in my opinion—I don't think a man is really gay until he needs the penis of the other man. So I knew from the very beginning that Zwi was without a doubt heterosexual. Not only did that not bother me in the least, it made our love all the more special.

My feelings for him mixed together various things. I thought: "Oh! I suddenly have a son! Or a younger brother." He put it into words: "I have no one else but you." With that he gave me the responsibility. But at the same time it was his manliness that I found so exciting!

From the start, I felt Zwi's playful naiveté in our relationship. Sometimes it seemed to me like a delayed pubescent encounter. On the one hand, I found that deeply touching. On the other hand, sexually, it wasn't enough for me in the long term. But our emotional bond has not broken to this day, even if I have long since ceased to be his helpful "older brother."

In the spring of 1943 I also met Hans-Oskar Löwenstein. He was sixteen at the time, like Zwi. We worked at the same construction site; I think it was somewhere in the Tiergarten district. We stood on the roof next to each other, carried tiles up there, and flirted.

Hans-Oskar was a fresh, inexperienced boy, in matters of the heart as well as in his appraisal of his status as a *mischling*. Sure, he had gone to a Jewish school and had been forced to perform slave labor and everything else, but no one in the Löwenstein–de Witt family, from the Charlottenburg district in the western part of the city, had ever felt seriously threatened so far. There had originally also been a baron's title in the Dutch part of their name, the part belonging to the maiden name of the Christian mother, but in the mid-1930s the family was stripped of its aristocratic title when Hanna Löwenstein refused to bow to pressure from the Nazis and divorce her Jewish husband. Some of their relatives were prominent people. Her sister Elisabeth Vosberg was the widow of the former mayor of Potsdam; she was a National Socialist from day one with a golden Nazi Party pin. But she didn't abandon her sister. A beautiful, privileged, pampered family.

Hans-Oskar didn't feel particularly at home on a construction site, and not only because it was hard work. He came from a wealthy family, and here he was surrounded by real Berlin proletarians. That was foreign to him. He also encountered even poorer Eastern European Jews, who were frowned upon by middle-class families—whether Jewish or "mixed"—in the western districts of the city. He found them despicable. Once he was absolutely repulsed as he told me about a little old Jew who was always making obscene remarks, what a horror. When he visited me at home for the first time, he was absolutely flabbergasted—it was my father! That really made me laugh.

Nevertheless, a little springtime romance developed between us. We went for a walk on Easter, reciting from *Faust*. It was a somewhat overbred romanticism compared to the swimming outing with Zwi. . . .

Hans-Oskar quickly knew what he wanted. Zwi, on the other hand, had seemed much younger, vulnerable, uncertain with intimacy. Hans-Oskar's charm manifested itself in overflowing enthusiasm. Our relationship was his "first big love," and he had to talk about it effusively everywhere he went. But even if he might have wished for it, first place was filled by Zwi. Luckily we never really had an argument about it, and Hans-Oskar and I remained friends.

Soon he took me home to his family and introduced me as his friend. Little by little, I integrated the Löwensteins into the efforts of our group, not because they needed help but because I suspected how much they could help us. With the Chug Chaluzi, Hans-Oskar suddenly got to know Jewish life, which was new to him. I didn't necessarily want to use him regarding confidential information, but he became active in Jizchak's "educational program." Some meetings took place at the Löwenstein home. I remember an evening of singing when Miriam and I once again tried singing two-part harmonies together. *Am Brunnen vor dem Tore*, "At the fountain at the gate" . . . it was really horrendous, but wonderful!

In June 1943 my mother received a letter from the hereafter—it came from Auschwitz-Birkenau. At the time we still didn't know exactly what was going on there, but we suspected, feared, guessed. Now, all of a sudden, we had it in black and white. My friend Karla Wagenberg had written the letter.

Although she was one of the first among us who supported our decision to oppose the deportations, she went along with a heavy heart when in early April she had received her lists at the *hachshara* in Neuendorf. The reason for her decision was a well-known dilemma; she felt she could neither take her younger sister into illegality with her nor let her go on the transport alone. They were both taken to Birkenau, where Karla was soon forced to play in the girls' orchestra. Or rather, she was "allowed" to play, for that is what helped her survive in the end.

Mustering all her "female cunning," she had talked an SS man into letting her send a birthday letter to her poor Aunt Hedwig, who was certainly worried sick about her. And she managed to encode the decisive message:

"You don't have to worry about me. Both of us are here and have work to do. How great that I learned to play the flute, for that has been my saving grace. We work in the kitchen. Life and work would be tolerable if there weren't always so much smoke around the chimney. . . ." She had written the word "chimney" in Hebrew letters with lots of hearts all around it—the SS man found that especially touching.

"Hundreds more come every day. We haven't given up hope of seeing you all again." As a postscript she added, "Many of us have already joined Alfred." She was referring to Alfred Selbiger, to make it clear to us that the transports to the east were synonomous with death. Now we knew without a doubt.

Our counterworld in Berlin became all the more important—in the underground, where it was possible, somehow, to survive. But we didn't have any illusions; we knew our lives were at risk. On the night of August 22, 1943, the Allied forces started heavy aerial bombing of the capital. They were flying raids more and more often during the day as well.

For our group, the bomb had already exploded, on June 17: Ewo—Edith Wolff—received a letter telling her to report to the command headquarters of the Gestapo!

We had a very hectic discussion. What could be the reason for the summons? Certainly, Ewo had increased her contacts with the circle around Franz Kaufmann and with Ernst Hallermann, Bertha Gerhardt, and other Christian helpers, as well as with those directly in danger. She took care of more and more people, arranging secret lodgings, food, ration cards, forged identity papers, and money. Some of the illegals worked, illegally of course. Considering the lack of workers due to the war, not many questions were asked. Others traded on the black market to get food and money, and many of the threads led back to Ewo. We tried to talk to her into going underground herself. But it was strange; although she worked day in and day out encouraging people to take this difficult step, and had even convinced her Jizchak to do it although it had not appealed to him at all, she still couldn't imagine doing it herself. On the other hand, she worried that the entire network of groups she worked together with could be exposed. She wanted to find out exactly what the Gestapo knew and to use her influence where she could. So she reported to the Gestapo on June 19.

"My dears! I am steadfast in my belief that all shall go well. However, if it must be, then I will take responsibility for all I have taken upon myself for our people and our work. The main thing is that we all remain unyield-ing: you on the outside and me on the inside, if it comes to that. As God wishes. Yours, Ewo."

She left that letter for us. Jizchak, Poldi, Zwi, and Ernst Hallermann accompanied her to Burgstrasse and then waited across the street in hopes that it would be only a short interrogation. But she didn't come back out. One—just one—of the many illegals she had taken care of had been caught with a forged food ration card. Under torture that woman, one of Jizchak's colleagues in western Germany, gave them Ewo's name. That was the be-ginning of Ewo's odyssey of suffering through seventeen camps and prisons until the end of the war.

In August, first Ernst Hallermann, then Franz Kaufmann, then, one after another, the other members of the Kaufmann circle were arrested. Günther Rogoff was able to escape to Switzerland, but during the brutal interrogations Poldi's and Zwi's names had been beaten out of the arrest-ees in connection with the sale of food ration cards. Jizchak was also on the Gestapo's list. But surprisingly, the Gestapo never found out about a group called Chug Chaluzi.

During her interrogation, Ewo told the officers a lot of things that they already must have known. They were "only" able to nail her on charges of forging documents, procuring false identity papers and food ration cards, and aiding and abetting Jews. Unceasingly, Nathan tried everything in his power to somehow get Ewo released.

As soon as Ewo was arrested, the Gestapo started pressuring her mother. Her connection to Jizchak Schwersenz was known, and they tried to get Frau Wolff to tell them where they could find him by promising that in return they would put Ewo in an ordinary jail instead of sending her to a concentration camp or prison.

In the fall of 1943 Ewo's tormented mother finally gave in. With a heavy heart, she betrayed Jizchak indirectly. An apartment where illegals— Jizchak, Rogoff, and others—often spent the night belonged to a Frau Lange, the Wolffs' former cleaning woman. Ewo's mother always met her at church on Sundays, where they chatted. That's all she told the Gestapo.

But that was enough. On October 2 Poldi was arrested there. It must have been terrible. He resisted desperately and was beaten to a pulp by the thugs. Displaying true Nazi cynicism, they had him held in the Jewish Hospital until he was well enough to be questioned, and then they "in-terrogated" him. After four weeks of torture, during which he kept silent, they sent him to his death in Auschwitz.

A marshal from the assembly camp on Grosse Hamburger Strasse brought us his final message: "I fought and didn't talk. Don't go back to the old quarters! Don't worry about me! I will remain brave and strong. God willing, we will see each other again."

THE LOSS OF EWO AND POLDI really hit us hard. Jizchak Schwersenz almost had a breakdown; first his friend Ewo, then one of the boys he loved the most. Little by little the noose was tightening around our necks. We had to find new hideouts, new ways to get food. Nathan Schwalb wrote regularly from Geneva telling us how "Aunt Gvula" was doing, that is, whether the border guards had been bribed to let refugees pass. Although we did not yet have any definite escape plans in the beginning of winter 1943–44, we told Nathan of our members who were at the greatest risk: the "full Jews," including Zwi and especially Jizchak. One of our Christian helpers, Luise Meier, a widow, also maintained contact with border guards, and a total of twenty-eight Jews had her to thank for their freedom.

Berlin was getting increasingly dangerous for all of us, since the Gestapo was installing more and more Jewish snatchers. One of the most notorious of them was the beautiful Stella Goldschlag, whom I knew slightly. She had avoided the Factory Operation and lived illegally for a short time but was arrested in the summer of 1943. Walter Dobberke from the Gestapo blackmailed her into working for them by threatening to send her parents, who were also under arrest, to a concentration camp. At first the Gestapo just wanted to get Günther Rogoff, the talented forger. Stella had known him since their school days together; he was one of her many admirers, and she had run into him on the street as late as spring 1943. But she didn't know that in the meantime he had escaped to Switzerland.

A victim forced to be a collaborator, at first she was used as bait to find Jews living in the underground. But Stella quickly became a merciless perpetrator. She showed increasing ambition as she hunted down illegals and had them arrested, usually accompanied by her fellow snatcher Rolf Isaaksohn. They were stars among the Gestapo's collection of informers and traitors.

And now, after Poldi had been caught in their trap, they were looking for the other "criminal" they had heard of—my Zwi. Once Poldi was arrested, it was Zwi who most urgently needed a new place to stay.

He remembered the address of the Communist that his coworker had given him on the day of the Factory Operation. Zwi had already been there once that summer, but the man was unable to help him at the time. "Maybe later," he had said. He kept his word. He let Zwi stay in his bungalow in the garden colony on Hönower Wiesenweg in Karlshorst.

In return for the accommodations, however, Zwi had to do something for the Communist Party. He was given a gun and had to distribute flyers in the S-Bahn—of course not directly to people, but he would leave a pile on a seat and they would distribute themselves. Zwi worked with another illegal, and they did good work, which was of course very dangerous. Others often simply threw the flyers away.

Then one evening in mid-November it happened. The Gestapo must have tortured Zwi's hiding place out of someone. They kicked in the door to the bungalow, and before Zwi even had a chance to think they had handcuffs on him. Two Jewish snatchers. Zwi was given the usual reception by the Gestapo. He was beaten and thrown in a cell. But he was very important to them as a possible informant, so they weren't about to transport him out right away.

They found next to nothing. Often when someone was snatched, notes or address books would reveal a lot of names—further victims. But Zwi didn't keep much. However, there were two things that were particularly aggravating. One was a piece of paper saying, "Margot Beck. Aschinger's at Rosenthaler Platz." That's where he had arranged to meet her once. The other was his "savings," which Frau Meier was going to use to pay for his escape. It cost four to five thousand marks to bribe the border guards, and Zwi had collected almost all of it. Now it was gone.

At his interrogation, Zwi was more clever than Poldi had been. He appeared incredibly talkative and told one fantastic story after another; he sometimes even took the officers to supposed meeting points where, unfortunately, no one showed up. . . . But he was beaten anyway. Perhaps less than if he had said nothing. Gestapo goons were brutal no matter what; he lost all his front teeth.

When Zwi got arrested, I almost lost my mind. The mere thought that he might follow Poldi . . . and Manfred. . . . I resolved to devote as much time as humanly possible to my illegal activities. We just had to make it, even if it seemed like everything was against us. Jizchak wrote to Nathan, "There is no Chug anymore."

I needed more time for the group. Every single day at the construction site—that just wouldn't do. I got along well with the site foreman. His name was Scheibler, and he was a simple, almost crude Berliner. But he had a weakness. Ever since one of his workers had fallen from the scaffolding and died, he had felt like a murderer and was constantly in a panic. "Kids, just make sure nothing happens to you while you're here," he would always say.

One day Mamsi picked me up from work, looking chic as ever. We had a plan. When she saw me up on the roof, she yelled at the man, "Are you crazy?! The boy up there, he's just a child. He could fall!" Scheibler simply answered, "Well, if you keep screaming like that, he's bound to fall!" But we knew we had made him nervous.

Act two followed a short time later. One winter day, after it had just snowed pretty heavily, I collapsed! No more strength! So now the little guy really had passed out; thank goodness he hadn't fallen from the top of the scaffolding. I was brought immediately to the Jewish Hospital. Of course they couldn't find anything wrong with me. But I got the doctor to write a statement saying I had "anemia." It sounded impressive and couldn't be proven or refuted all too easily. When I reported back to the construction site three days later, Scheibler listened to the diagnosis thoughtfully. "Could happen again, huh?" He rubbed his chin. "Then take good care of yourself, kid." From then on, whenever I had something more important to do than clear away rubble, I simply wouldn't go to work. I had a ready excuse—anemia!

The circumstances under which Zwi got free belong to the most adventurous stories of our very adventurous ways of survival. He was in a cell in the camp on Grosse Hamburger Strasse, where prisoners were ten to a cell and slept on bunk beds. Old men, young men, children. We knew some of them, such as the father, son, and daughter in the Zajdmann family, who had also belonged to the Chug. They had been caught by Stella Goldschlag and Rolf Isaaksohn in the state opera house on Unter den Linden. Only the mother had gotten away. Zwi and the Zajdmanns started plotting immediately; they wanted to chance an escape.

Next to the cell there was a room with air raid tools—hoes, shovels, picks. With these tools it would be possible to break open the bars on the windows, Zwi thought as soon as he saw the room. The grating consisted of individual iron bars welded together. It was anchored to the window frame with cement. The windows were partially underground, facing out onto a pathway at the back of the building, away from the street. Patrols went up and down at regular intervals, and even at night it was lit up like daylight. Beyond the pathway was the Jewish cemetery, surrounded by a sturdy chain-link fence. One day Zwi noticed that someone had cut a hole into the fence—the escape route!

In the final days of 1943 the air raids by the Allies were increasing in number. All prisoners had to leave their cells and go into the corridor, where they were guarded by a policeman. Since the tools from the air raid cellar were needed, the door, which was normally locked, was opened momentarily. Zwi grabbed himself a pick and hid it under his bed.

The next day four of the prisoners hooked the pick onto the welded joints on the bars and heaved them apart. There was an incredible clang as the grating loosened, and at first they were really scared, hearts pounding, sweating. The grating was quickly propped back into place, and no one came to check. They decided to try it for real on New Year's Eve, a few days later, since most of the guards would likely have other things on their minds. Luckily the aerial bombing that December 31, 1943, was especially heavy, so of course the lights above the pathway were turned off. The escapees crawled out, one after the other.

As Esther Zajdmann was about to climb out, a small boy who was just returning to the cell said loudly in the corridor: "Look, they're escaping through the window!" The guards responded amazingly fast and managed to catch Esther. Her father Abram and brother Moritz were already gone.

Zwi raced off with Moritz. They hurried through the cemetery with bombers hammering overhead. At the other side of the cemetery they crossed the street. There they ran right into the arms of a police officer, who started cursing and scolding when he saw them: "What are you doing out here? You should be in an air raid shelter. Are you crazy?"

Moritz knew of a place in Neukölln, in the south of Berlin, where they could go. It was another garden colony bungalow. They stayed there a few days. But it got colder and colder, and they had next to nothing to eat. The air raids never let up. Zwi told me later about one night when they almost went crazy. Bombs were exploding all over; nearby an antiaircraft unit was shooting incessantly. They were lying on the floor under a bed, holding their ears and screaming and crying like little children. The next morning they left the bungalow and went their separate ways.

I never did understand why the Gestapo waited so long to follow up on Zwi's note with Miriam's name on it. But now, since Zwi was among the New Year's Eve escapees, they pursued every possible lead. The new year was still not very old, and snatcher Rolf Isaaksohn was standing at our door. "Does a Margot Beck live here?"

Miriam got an incredible fright.

"With whom do you have a meeting at Aschinger's at Rosenthaler Platz? With Abrahamssohn? And when?"

Miriam didn't know anything. She acted very friendly and shy, helpful and unsuspecting. Yes, of course she would go with him to the restaurant.

Isaaksohn dragged her there numerous times, of course in vain. But at least we now knew that Zwi had broken out, since they were looking for him again. Of course he would make sure not to turn up at Aschinger's.

The first time he came, Isaaksohn saw me as well. I was sitting at the table in the next room writing a letter to Nathan Schwalb, of all people. When I heard Isaaksohn come in, I decided to continue what I was doing, as though nothing was up. It would only be more obvious if I suddenly stopped writing and started putting things away. As he and Miriam walked past my open door to leave, the snatcher asked, "Who's in there?"

I'll never forget Miriam's presence of mind. "Oh, that's just my brother. Forget him; he's always writing poems." Chutzpah prevails!

Aside from my sister, I deliberately didn't involve anyone from my family in the illegal activities. With one exception—Uncle Willi, Aunt Trude's husband.

He had been shot to pieces in World War I and was hard of hearing on top of that, so he wasn't very useful to the Nazis anymore. They left him alone, and he didn't even have to join the Nazi party.

But then he was indeed called up. They made him a guard soldier in work camps. One day in the winter of 1943–44, when he was home on leave, he came over to me. "Männe," he said (he still called me by my baby name), "we have to talk. I'm a guard at a women's work camp in the Harz mountains. There are some Jewish girls from Vienna there." Our voices got more and more agitated and at the same time secretive. It didn't take long until Uncle Willi became a courier between that camp and Berlin, and other places too; I forwarded the letters.

That was yet one more connection that was supported through Nathan's network. The girls received glucose from Switzerland. Later, glucose was even sent to Auschwitz-Birkenau. Uncle Willi serves as an example of the great difference between police, SS, Gestapo, and soldiers. The soldiers were sometimes among the most humane of the guards, though they often lacked the courage to do anything against the terrible injustice they witnessed. But many made an effort to ease the fate of the prisoners, if only through such courier services.

Once I knew that Zwi had escaped, I could not stay calm for a second. Where was the little devil? I was terribly worried. I sulked. Since he hadn't turned up at our place, he could only be hiding at Marie Grünberg's, his aunt from Blankenburg. She had already hidden her Jewish brother-in-law in a small stone house in a garden colony. But I didn't have her address. All I had were bits of information.

She rode a bicycle. She wore thick glasses. She was married to a Jewish man and had to pick up her food ration cards at the Jewish card office. That was one of the inconceivable administrative paradoxes. Berlin was officially considered *judenrein*, but there was still an office for Jewish food ration cards for the remaining *mischlings*. My friend Mamsi had an idea. "When I pick up my cards, I go to the office in Pankow—that's the same district as Blankenburg! Aunt Marie must go there too." I described the aunt to Mamsi, and on January 24, the next pickup day (the cards were distributed monthly), we made our way to the office. First Mamsi did a shift, waiting for hours until noon. Then I was there from noon until three P.M., when the card office closed.

Can you believe it, at five minutes to three a woman with thick glasses pedaled up on a bicycle and walked in! I followed. As I went past her I whispered, "Aunt Marie?!" "Go away! Go away!" she hissed, then added, "Yes, he's with me!" I turned around furtively. "Zwi's birthday is in three days. I want to see him." "Okay, take the last bus," she responded, "to the last stop in Pankow!"

I have seldom awaited a "rendezvous" with such a pounding heart. On January 27, 1944, I stood at the bus stop and waited for my Zwi. I had a pair of pajamas with me as a birthday present. No idea where I got them from.

The last bus came, and four people got out. No Zwi. I was feeling desperate. What could have happened? What should I do? The people started walking away, and there was nothing else for me to do but to take off too. I was dragging along the main street. An old man was standing in a doorway, one of the people who had gotten off the bus. Ugly, wearing a long winter coat and a hat. I had already walked past him when it finally clicked. That was Zwi! I didn't even recognize him with his front teeth missing. I have never forgotten that image, the shadow standing in the doorway. . . .

There was a similar silhouette in a picture in the exhibition "Jews in the Resistance" in 1993 in Berlin. The organizers had chosen a dark, bluish photograph of a large man with a hat for the exhibition poster. When Zwi saw it he smiled and said, "That was your idea, wasn't it, Gad?" Only then did I realize: Yes, that's just how he had looked back then.

"Puppe," the little doll, and "Männe," the little man, 1925. Photograph from the private archives of Gad Beck, Berlin.

Three sisters: Hedwig, Frieda, and Trude Kretschmar, 1927. Photograph from the private archives of Gad Beck, Berlin.

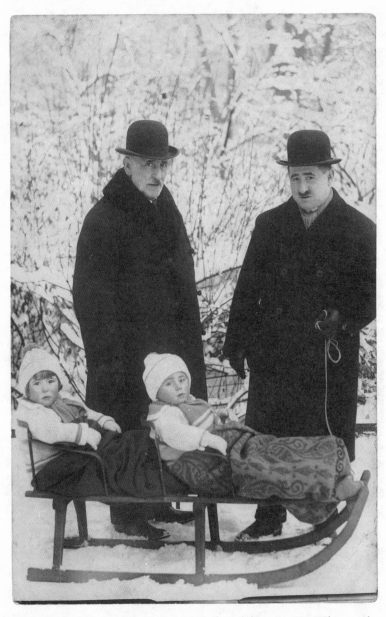

Reuwen Beck of Vienna, his son Heinrich Beck, and the twins, 1924. Photograph from the private archives of Miriam Rosenberg, Holon, Israel.

Top: Schulz's Bakery, later Kneifel's, at Prenzlauer Strasse 12a.
Bottom: At the Pastry-Cooks' Ball, 1926: *left front,* Heinrich Beck; *next to him,* Hedwig Beck. Photographs from the private archives of Gad Beck, Berlin.

Top: At Obersee Park, 1931: *left to right,* Uncle Willi, Mother, Father, Aunt Martha; *in front,* Gerhard and Margot.
Bottom: Gerhard and Margot, 1937. Photographs from the private archives of Miriam Rosenberg, Holon, Israel.

Five sisters and their husbands, in Teltow, 1939: *top*, Frieda, Martha, Anna, Hedwig, Trude; *bottom,* Telesfor, Wobbi, Paul, Heinrich, Willi. Photographs from the private archives of Miriam Rosenberg, Holon, Israel.

Left: Cousin Inge. Photograph from the private archives of Miriam Rosenberg, Holon, Israel.
Right: "Mamsi." Photograph from the private archives of Gad Beck, Berlin.

Top: The last meeting of the Youth Aliyah leadership, 1941: *far left,* Lotte Kaiser; fourth from left, Sonja Okun, *behind and to her right,* Alfred Selbiger.
Bottom: In the Lewin household in the Scheunenviertel, 1941: *from right,* Herr Lewin, Manfred Lewin, Jizchak Schwersenz, Rudi Lewin, Schlomo Lewin, and other members of the Lewin family. Photographs from the private archives of Jizchak Schwersenz, Berlin.

Manfred Lewin, 1941. Photograph from the private archives of Jizchak Schwersenz, Berlin.

Top: Edith Wolff, called Ewo, around 1938.
Bottom: Jizchak Schwersenz, as "the Aryan Heinz Joachim" in the forged passport of Ernst Hallermann, September 1942. Photographs from the private archives of Jizchak Schwersenz, Berlin.

Top: The Chug Chaluzi in Grunewald Forest, 1943: *from left,* Gad Beck, David Billard, Jizchak Schwersenz, Zwi Abrahamssohn, Poldi Chones.
Bottom: At the Sukkoth party at the Beck's, 1943: *from left,* Gad Beck, Jizchak Schwersenz, Ewo (hidden), Zwi Abrahamssohn, Poldi Chones, David Billard, Miriam Beck. Photographs from the private archives of Jizchak Schwersenz, Berlin.

Miriam Beck, the "elegant mistress of a Swiss diplomat." Photograph from the private archives of Miriam Rosenberg, Holon, Israel.

Zwi Abrahamssohn. Photograph from the private archives of Zwi Aviram, Holon, Israel.

Hans-Oskar Löwenstein. Photograph from the private archives of Gad Beck, Berlin.

On Lake Havel, 1946: *from left:* Hanna Löwenstein, Lea Jacob, Paul Safirstein, Gretel Tiedemann, Hans-Oskar Löwenstein, Horst Wollert, Fritz Löwenstein, Vera Müller. Photograph from the private archives of Hans-Oskar Löwenstein, Berlin.

Nathan Schwalb and Jizchak Schwersenz in Switzerland, 1944. Photograph from the private archives of Jizchak Schwersenz, Berlin.

5

I N EARLY FEBRUARY 1944 Jizchak Schwersenz escaped to Switzerland.
Herbert Strunck, a corporal at the Staaken military airfield, had gotten him the forged identity papers. Crossing the border to Switzerland was arranged with the help of Luise Meier. Strunck, who would later
play a major role for our entire group, was too daring for Frau Meier. At
a meeting with her, he and Jizchak fantasized about a mass escape in munitions vehicles. For this reason, she gradually withdrew from our group;
unfortunately, that didn't help her much. After two other refugees she had
helped were caught in May, the Gestapo arrested her as well.

Jizchak took the train to the border zone. It was a nerve-wracking journey, we later heard. He and the woman Strunck arranged to accompany him
were subjected to constant ID-card controls. They finally crossed the border
at an unpatrolled point after hiking for hours, only to be arrested in Schaff-
hausen on February 13 on charges of espionage. The local Jewish Community was able to straighten out the misunderstanding quickly, and a few
days later Jizchak Schwersenz and Nathan Schwalb met for the first time.

This was an important moment because it gave all of us hope that other
members of Chug Chaluzi could successfully escape to Switzerland as well.
Jizchak reported on our work and gave Nathan a list with twenty names,
the most active members of the group. They were put on the Swiss foreign
police's "list of refugees not to be refused entry."

Now they had to decide where relief packages from Switzerland could
be sent. That meant news, food, medication, and especially money. The
Hechalutz was receiving more and more donations from Jewish organizations in the United States. Jizchak mentioned a few possible addresses.

The first was one of his favorite boys, Günther Davidowicz, whom
we called Arje. The eighteen-year-old Arje had always been very close to

Jizchak, and obviously they stayed in touch now too. He wrote letters to Arje, and not very prudent ones, boasting about "large sums" that were now available.

But Arje was involved with a girl from our group named Margot (a different Margot, not my sister), and she was pregnant. That complicated their situation considerably. They lived with her Christian mother, who was very careful to keep her distance from the Jewish-Zionist activities.

Nathan's messenger, a Zurich jeweler named Gübelin, was allowed to travel back and forth between the two countries because he was a courier for the Swiss embassy. When he knocked at the Davidowicz door in late March with the first large amount of money, Arje's mother sent him away immediately. She didn't want anything to do with it. So much for Jizchak's first choice.

The second name on the list was Else Szimke. She was a typical Berliner house superintendent, who had her fingers in all kinds of semilegal or entirely crooked deals. She rented single rooms of her apartment on Alte Schützenstrasse, right behind Alexanderplatz, to prostitutes. She also dealt in food and ration cards on the black market and hid illegals now and then. Even Jizchak had stayed at her place for a while.

The Szimkes took care of a building whose Jewish owner had been kicked out. In Berlin most building supers were either absolute Nazis or friendly to Jews. Frau Szimke was definitely no Nazi; the main thing on her mind was making a good deal. In time she became one of our main sources of food from the black market; she really exploited us, but we could nevertheless count on her. Her husband was a long-distance trucker who was deferred from military service because of a hernia. Their past revealed traces of Communism, and all things considered, they were okay.

Else Szimke was a warmhearted and rather crude middle-aged woman. She wore a bun, was a little plump, and had the clever though otherwise unobtrusive facial expression of a working-class woman. She talked a lot and was quick-witted and outspoken.

Every time—and I mean *every* time—I was at her place, she would tell me just *how* she slept with her husband. When she got married, she discovered a single lying-down position she liked—with her legs wrapped around his—and she never changed. She'd throw herself on the couch to demonstrate—at least her half of it. Actually, she just wanted to show someone she considered distinguished (me!) how she had sex. Now, she was pretty strong, but he was a real bull. It must have been a real mega-merger! In short, we would sometimes talk about intimate things, like two good girlfriends. Throughout my life I have developed friendly, trusting relationships more quickly with women than with men, precisely because I am not physically attracted to women. With men it was usually the other way around. If I was not attracted to them physically, then it was difficult for me to develop trust and friendship.

Szimke was typical of a certain type of Berliner, especially common in the eastern districts, who had a strong, almost vulgar, Berlin accent. These people could really put on airs. When they got all dressed up and went to a café on Kurfürstendamm, they would fumble around with their cigarette or coffee cup as if they were sitting at a table with the Kaiser. That's how artificial and contrived it would look. Or they would put on a hat and explain with pursed lips, "Oh, yes! The other day we were on Unter den Linden!" But as soon as they opened their mouths, the same old torrent would come flowing out. They couldn't help it; that's how they were. It was horrendous. But sweet as well. I find that irresistible about the Berliners. And Szimke, well, she was one of them.

So now the courier went to her. After he had explained why he was there, she was a little too eager to collect the money. "Okay then, hand it over." That made the man suspicious. It wasn't all that easy after all. So he came to us, the third address on his list.

First he had trouble even finding our apartment. A bomb had destroyed the staircase in the front part of the building, so you had to go up the back stairs, but of course he didn't know that. Finally he stood in the middle of the courtyard and shouted, "Hedwig! Hedwig!" My mother heard him, totally surprised. Who was this man she didn't know?

He didn't waste any words once he had located her in the building. He wanted to talk to me. As usual, I wasn't there. He said he was from the Swiss embassy. They quickly figured out what was going on, and by the time I came home he was already gone. And my dear parents were sitting there counting out a hundred thousand marks!

That was immense wealth for us. I had to think of how Zwi hadn't been able to escape because he was short a measly five hundred marks for Frau Meier. Now there was enough money. Nathan Schwalb had even enclosed a citizenship certificate issued by the Republic of El Salvador for Ewo. But Ewo's mother didn't dare to use it for fear that Ewo might get into even more trouble.

From now on, connections to the Hechalutz office in Geneva, cash payments, and other means of support all went through the Swiss embassy, which made it possible to help not only members of Chug Chaluzi survive the war but many others as well who were living illegally and had nothing to do with the Chug.

Up to that point, Nathan's letters had always come by regular mail, which meant they had passed through at least one censorship office. Now letters started coming by courier, so Nathan was able to express some things in far greater detail. But he continued to "encode" parts of the information in Hebrew.

His first letter delivered by courier was written on March 18, 1944. He wrote:

Try, as J. [Jizchak] did, to talk with Hatzalah [rescue]. Connect her with all the sisters and brothers according to Reshimah [the list of Chug members that Jizchak had taken with him to Switzerland]. Help everyone regardless of their relationship [regardless of whether they are "full Jews" or *mischlings*], and greet everyone warmly from dear Yetziah [rescue]. You should also send my love especially to Herbert, Eva W. [two illegal friends of the group from Nordhausen in the Harz mountains], and Edith W. [Ewo] because of the enclosed darkiah [citizenship certificate]. If Edith is not yet babeit [home, i.e., has not yet been released], then send her the darkiah in the best way possible. It would be better if she were to visit Bricha [to try to escape]. But if she is babeit, then E., like all from the Reshimah, should visit Joachim soon in Kivutzot [escape to Switzerland in small groups]. Gvula [border] is okay and understanding. . . .

Anochi [I] repeats once again that the mea elef [100,000 marks] is for Bricha [escape] according to Reshimah and Esra Nistar [to support those in hiding]. Please talk to Joachim's chaver [Schwersenz's friend Strunck] in the Neyar matter [false papers] immediately and send him and Frau Gerhardt warm greetings from J. Send detailed answer via shal [courier] and confirm matanah [the shipment].

All of Nathan's letters were that personal. It is hard to imagine how he kept track of things. From Geneva he planned numerous rescue operations and kept up international contacts, and he still managed to write about two dozen such letters every day. They were often the only shimmer of hope for the recipients, threatened by the Nazis, their backs against the wall.

Nathan's letters contained more and more new names. This is why: Jews who had emigrated to Switzerland or the United States had contacted the Hechalutz because they were worried about their relatives stuck in Berlin and elsewhere. Nathan then moved heaven and earth to find out where the people were and to help them. Those were the names I received. They had avoided the transports, had gone into hiding, and were in need of help.

Sometimes the addresses didn't even exist anymore; the houses had been bombed out, so the people had gone underground. When I would approach them they were skeptical, to put it mildly. No wonder! I mean, who was I? So Miriam and I made a plan. It involved her fur coat! Hard to believe she had one, but she did. Through one of my aunts, my mother had gotten hold of a ration coupon for a winter coat, and Miriam needed one desperately. They went to the Tietz department store at Alexanderplatz and looked at the meager selection. The saleswoman was helpful, but there wasn't much she could do.

As they were turning to go, my mother sighed and said, "Oh, you know, we're not used to being spoiled nowadays anyway. We're Jews, you see. . . ."

"What are you?" the woman stopped in her tracks and started smiling. "Then I got something here for the girl!" And she reached into a closet and pulled out a fur coat. Miriam still wore it ten years later in Israel.

To go with the fur, we managed to get shoes with wedged heels that were especially chic, and we dressed me up as well—thanks to the Swiss contacts—in diplomatic style, with stuff you couldn't find in Germany at that time: a suit, pigskin briefcase, shoes with crepe soles. The courier brought me everything. Then I got a passport of a stateless person under the name of Günther Kaplan (the true holder is still alive today, living in Munich). So we often went together to the addresses of the Jews living in hiding. I was with my mistress—of course all diplomats had mistresses; that made an impression and created trust. I always said I was from the Swiss embassy so they wouldn't think I was a Gestapo trap. At some point they were willing to accept help, whether it was food or plans for a possible escape. I couldn't promise them very much, but at least I could confirm that they were alive and well and pass the information on to Nathan.

These illegals were not supposed to know anything about our Chug Chaluzi group. They certainly would not have been able to withstand a Gestapo interrogation. The two worlds were to some extent mutually exclusive. Zwi, for example, never met these people.

In order to make arrangements with Nathan's couriers, for cash transfers and the like, there was yet another contact person, who came neither from me nor from the embassy. Her name was Helga Ammann, and she was the Christian secretary of a German industrial spy who traveled back and forth between Berlin and Switzerland. She was also the lover of Nathan's courier Gübelin. I have no idea how they recruited that woman. Maybe she thought it was glamorous and exciting to live the life of a grande dame during the war; maybe she felt like Mata Hari or something. One can assume she was critical of the Nazi regime. But in any case, this was her way to avoid mundane life and move in higher circles. Mistress of a VIP, secret agent—that was romantic and sophisticated at the same time.

I was supposed to stay in contact with this secretary–secret agent so Gübelin would be able to reach me. My relationship with Helga fluctuated back and forth between gallantry and almost cheeky flirtation. She was a very elegant woman, a spoiled little rich girl; I had never met anyone like her before. She lived in a four-room apartment on Brandenburgische Strasse in the western part of Berlin, and she never went into an air raid shelter. Someone had told her that the reinforced door leading from her kitchen to the back staircase was the safest possible place to be in an air raid, so that's where she always sat. Sometimes, when the sirens sounded while I was in her apartment, we would squat knee to knee, a somewhat grotesque form of a cultured coffee klatch.

You see, we always had coffee. It was never a hasty cash transfer but instead a sophisticated visit, almost like in old times. Sometimes her boss, the spy, came too. He thought I was someone with connections to the Swiss embassy. That could have developed into a delicate, and embarrassing, situation. He knew Switzerland; I didn't. Every street name in Zurich or Geneva was absolute blind flying for me. Luckily, he liked to hear himself talk and the answers weren't very important. She would bring me to the door and press the bag with the money into my hand or, if that would have been too obvious, discreetly ask that I come back the next day.

Gübelin had told her all about our activities. Sometimes she even got food for us or held on to large sums of money temporarily; in other words, she wasn't only a middle-person, she sometimes took great risks. In return for that, Gübelin demanded that Nathan get her out of Germany at some point. That happened in the fall of 1944.

Although Helga's boss was a spy for Germany, he seemed to be more of an opportunist than a hard-core Nazi. She hinted a few times that even if he found out about us it wouldn't have been a problem. But we never had to put him to the test; he didn't find out about us.

I made Hans-Oskar's father my minister of finance. We really needed all the money that came from Switzerland, but of course not all at once. It had to be kept somewhere, and Fritz Löwenstein became our financial courier and banker, so to speak. For someone like me, who came from a family where we couldn't manage money all that well—not to mention such large sums—Löwenstein was really impressive. He was a stock market expert for the Commerzbank. He had to know something about money!

I couldn't think of anyone better. My simple Aunt Frieda would have been so afraid she'd have peed in her pants. Uncle Wobbi might have taken on the task, but his daughter Ingelies had acquired a rare glandular disorder, and the whole family was living on tenterhooks; that wouldn't have worked.

At first I had to garnish the whole thing with a few lies . . . I had to go away the next day, and could he watch a few "valuables" for me? For security reasons, I didn't want to tell the Löwensteins the whole story right away. But Hans-Oskar's parents had played along from the very beginning and were immediately willing to take on the responsibility. Whenever I needed money he would pack a few thousand marks in with the sandwiches for his morning break when he went to work. If a new shipment came, I would bring a full bag to him. He would put it in a safe place until the next time I needed money. I never asked where he kept it.

It was not until after the war that I found out what his clever wife had thought of. She hid our Swiss money in the villa of her Nazi-sister Elisabeth in Potsdam! Nothing could have been safer. . . .

I TRIED TO KEEP MY PARENTS from getting involved, except for Nathan's letters, which he still sent to my mother. I had long since stopped using our attic to hide my illegals. I never forgot how much my father was opposed to my "Zionist activities"; and I preferred being able to relax now and then with my family—my parents, my aunts—precisely because they were not directly involved in our work. Besides, in the spring of 1944 they had enough problems of their own to worry about.

Since our apartment was only accessible from the back stairway across the courtyard, my parents had more and more encounters with a slightly paranoid Nazi woman who lived in that back building and never liked us anyway. Around Easter 1944 she started throwing little packages against our kitchen window from her apartment every day. They would land inside if the window was open. Wrapped up neatly in newspaper was . . . shit. On the newspaper, she would scribble "Jew whore" or some other abusive words. My mother felt really harassed by it.

She talked with the aunts about what she could do. They even suggested their going to the woman: "What if we go to her, we Christians, and give her a thrashing? What could she do?" But it never did come to any kind of organized resistance, since my mother simply couldn't take it anymore.

One beautiful day, my mother came home from shopping carrying a milk can. She met the Nazi woman on the staircase and had to listen to her vile obscenities again. My mother raised her arm and hit the old woman over the head with the can. Not only that, she pushed her down the steps too!

Once she realized what she had done, my mother ran down to Frau Szczepanski on the ground floor and told her what had happened before the crazy neighbor had a chance to recover. All Frau Szczepanski had to say was "Get your tail out of here quick, girl, before she calls the police!"

While they were still talking, my father came home, and they quickly went up to the apartment to discuss what they should do. Even today, their decision is hard to comprehend. They decided to turn themselves in!

"But I did something wrong," my mother said. You have to imagine the lunacy. The neighbor didn't even file a report. My parents went together to the police station at Alexanderplatz and reported themselves. Compared to the Gestapo, the police were harmless and friendly, and they talked it over calmly. "Aha, so you have a mixed marriage? But you are a Christian?" they said to my mother. "Yes." "Okay, but we'll at least have to get a statement," one of them finally said, somewhat at a loss.

At that moment, my mother told us later, another one joined them, glanced at their papers, and said, "They're Jews! Are you crazy? Send them off to Grosse Hamburger Strasse!"

After that, everything went very fast. My parents were separated in the assembly camp. My mother stayed there; my father was sent to the Sachsenhausen concentration camp. An absolutely unfathomable story. Miriam and I tried to figure out what we could do. We couldn't think of any way to save our parents. The only thing that was certain was that, considering all our activities, we could not stay in the apartment on Prenzlauer Strasse, though we rarely showed up there anyway. Miriam moved in with her best friend, Ursel Littmann, who lived near Friedrichshain park. They worked together washing railroad cars. For me, there were other places where I could stay temporarily.

A few days later, when I was on my way to Frau Szczepanski, I saw an elderly man walking down the street about twenty meters ahead of me. Hey, I thought, isn't that the former police inspector who has been friends with my father for ages!? Even after we had started wearing the yellow star, this man continued to be friendly to my father and greet him on the street. I walked up next to him and whispered, "Excuse me, but I have to speak with you." "Yes, okay, come into the entranceway, but not too close."

Okay. He looked around quickly to see if anyone had seen us, then took me up to his apartment and asked what the matter was. I told him the story with my parents. He shook his head and said, "There's probably not a whole lot to be done." Just as flabbergasted as the rest of us, he started pacing up and down in his living room, thinking. He kept on shaking his head in disbelief. Finally he simply said, "I'll try something."

Then he went right over to his desk. He got out an old piece of stationery, complete with letterhead—Germans like official letterheads—name, office, etc., and he wrote a letter. "To the commandant of the Sachsenhausen concentration camp. . . . The Jew Heinrich Beck was admitted to your camp. He is married to a Christian. . . ." He continued that he had known Beck since 1918 and that Beck had always been an upright citizen, often helping him clear up cases and always working to support law and order in our district. "I believe it is out of the question that this man could have done anything wrong." Then he requested that all necessary steps be taken for the release of Heinrich Beck. Yours sincerely, etc. etc.

My mother and the actual event were not mentioned at all in the letter. "I don't know if this will help," he said as I left, "but I wish you luck." I threw the letter into the closest mailbox.

Nothing happened in the following weeks; at least that's what I thought. Much later I found out that Frau Szczepanski and Kneifel the baker had gotten together to go to the police station at Alexanderplatz to submit a statement in support of my parents. And the wheels of bureaucracy continued to turn.

In the meantime, I tried to get in contact with my mother through the marshals at the camp on Grosse Hamburger Strasse. I wanted at least to hear how she was doing and if she was even still there. . . . For all I knew, she could have been deported! But I couldn't find out anything. We got no news from her and even less from my father.

Then, that summer, my father was released after having spent three and a half months in Sachsenhausen! He never said a word about that time of his life, what he experienced there, how it happened that he was released. He never said a word and we never asked. One day he was simply let out.

And what did this fool do? Instead of staying as far away as possible from all representatives of the authorities, the very first thing he did was to go to Grosse Hamburger Strasse. Hard to believe. He went in waving his release certificate. And my mother was let out too. If they released the Jew, then they had to release the Christian as well! So in no time they were both back sitting in their apartment on Prenzlauer Strasse. My father reported to his job the next day, excusing himself for his absence. He presented his release certificate, saying he hadn't been at work because he was in a concentration camp. Only in Germany. . . .

My Christian relatives had come a long way. Their fears from the early war years that caused them to become more distanced from us had totally disappeared since the demonstrations against the Factory Operation in 1943. They had learned something unheard-of for your basic respectable bourgeois citizen, that is, to take a political stand in opposition to the authorities. Their sense of belonging, of family, and of sticking together managed to prevail over the ingrained German principle of unconditional obedience to authority.

When my parents were imprisoned in spring 1944, it was my relatives who organized new accommodations for me. Uncle Telesfor had a great-nephew, Leo Neumann. Although a soldier, Leo was in a poor state of health, so he worked in Berlin in the supply department of the Wehrmacht. His wife and child had been evacuated to East Prussia.

When hearing about the milk-can incident and its consequences, Leo had said, "Our apartment is empty most of the time. I'm hardly ever there. I can give Gad the key."

The apartment was on Greifswalder Strasse. I lived there officially as a relative of Leo's. He brought me there and said, "You can sleep in the small room. In fact, I'd really like that."

I didn't understand. He pointed to a photograph of a man. It was his brother. "He committed suicide at a very young age, in his early thirties." I waited for an explanation. "He was like you." No, Leo didn't mean blond, and he didn't mean Jewish. He couldn't say "the word." It was too difficult for him.

The apartment became a small central office for our group, and now and again I let friends sleep there if things got tight. First and foremost, Zwi.

After his escape he had stayed outside Berlin for a while with Bertha Gerhardt, the secondary school teacher, but one day she sent him to me with a letter. "If you want to help your friend, get him a quarter pound of butter and milk every day. He has TB and needs constant nourishment. I can't take on the responsibility." Well, that was great news! All the problems were doubled if an illegal got sick. Now it was even my Zwi. It had been hard enough to get his knocked-out front teeth replaced.

There was always a lot going on in the apartment. Whenever there was an air raid, there were a number of options. Hans-Oskar, who visited often, would disappear immediately. He usually managed to catch the S-Bahn from the Weissensee station right around the corner and go back to his family in Charlottenburg. The rest of us usually ran to a large mass shelter at the S-Bahn station. That seemed more inconspicuous to us.

Zwi and I often saw a man there who—according to rumor—had been deferred from military service because he was an engineer involved in research and was therefore important. He looked great, and the women were all crazy about him—no wonder, with such a shortage of men around. They would give him cigarettes till he had them coming out of his ears. He was generally very friendly to us, but I was careful. He observed everything very closely—too closely.

One day Leo came to me with a worried look on his face and said, "Gad, my wife is coming back from East Prussia!" It was getting too precarious for her there with the baby, and they were already on their way back to Berlin. That meant I had to leave the apartment. "I know what that means for you and your friends. Believe me, I'll try my best; maybe I can find something else."

It wasn't long before he told me about a man I should go talk to. It was the engineer from the shelter! Paul Dreyer had been able to avoid becoming a member of the Nazi Party, either despite or because of his high-ranking position. Instead he had joined the NSKK, the National Socialist Motorist Corps, like my Uncle Paul. This small peripheral organization was generally left alone by the Nazi bigwigs. It evidently sufficed in giving its members the appearance of being loyal to the party line without having to commit themselves to anything.

Dreyer worked for the Bell chemical company, which, by the way, was never bombed because it was partly owned by the Americans. At the front gate I offered a sharp "Heil Hitler" and asked for Engineer Dreyer. The doorman answered in a friendly tone. "He's upstairs, but with him you can forget about your Nazi salute!"

"Oh, there's little Günther Kaplan," Dreyer greeted me amiably. Then he got very serious. He looked at me and said, "Either you're a Jew or you're gay!" That gave me a real start, and I said cautiously, trying to keep my composure, "I'm sorry, I don't understand what you mean, Herr Dreyer." He got up and walked over to a cabinet, pulling out five receipts I had written that were signed by a Frau Kristella, one of the illegals I was helping.

I didn't figure out the connection until later. One of Kristella's two sons had escaped to Switzerland and, through Nathan, arranged for us to help her. Thus the confirmed receipts for money. The other son was living in the underground with her. The son who escaped had been Dreyer's lover, and now Dreyer was helping the mother and the remaining son as best he could.

Frau Kristella had given Dreyer the money and the receipts for safe-keeping, since his safe was of course a better hiding place than her lodgings. Whenever she needed money, he would take it out of the safe for her. She was also the cleaning woman for Strunck, the corporal who had helped Jizchak and her first son escape. Sometimes coincidences have their own sense of inner logic.

Paul Dreyer didn't beat around the bush. After he made it clear that he knew about my illegal activities, he opened up himself and told me about his lost love. "I know I will never experience a love like that again," he stated soberly. "Well . . . so you need an apartment?"

In no time the situation had changed totally. Leo had said I was Günther Kaplan, a young acting student who'd been deferred from military service because he was suspected of having tuberculosis and who needed an apartment. Incidentally, that's why I always went around wearing a bit of makeup at that time. I thought that's what actors did. How should I have known that Frau Kristella had long since told him about our group? I could speak openly with Paul Dreyer.

He told me about his secretary, Elly Peipe, who was willing to make her apartment available as a hiding place for illegals. She was a widow and had moved in with relatives. Dreyer had the key to her old apartment, which I could have immediately, and there was even coal in the basement for heating.

We went there directly: Utrechter Strasse 50, in the Wedding district. Frau Peipe's one-room apartment was on the ground level in the back building, through the courtyard. It was furnished in a terribly charming manner, in lilac and pink, with landscapes of blooming heather on the walls. I found the atmosphere stifling. But the rent was only twenty-seven marks per month. Actually, it was perfect for us. Frau Peipe didn't even charge us any more than she had to pay herself—she could have charged us a hundred times more! How often had I encountered people who made a killing off our desperate situation! Once we started getting money from Switzerland we were in a position to pay exorbitant prices if we really had to. But Elly Peipe didn't need to be bribed; she took on the risk of her own accord.

Paul Dreyer made me agree to two conditions. First, only I could live in the apartment, no one else. That was tough. In the apartment on Greifswalder Strasse I was constantly putting people up if lodging was needed on short notice. Or if I wanted to have a tiny drop of private life— with Zwi or others.

That was not allowed in the Utrechter Strasse apartment. But Dreyer's thoughts were definitely also horizontal in nature. The second condition was that he could come by regularly. . . . At first I was shocked at the bluntness with which he made his demand. But I didn't have much time to waste. I agreed.

Dreyer lived with his mother. He told her he had to do air raid patrol at the factory, as a pretext, on the evenings when he came to "visit." Instead he would come with bread and ham, and anything else he was able to get, to collect my love services. Over the next few months, he did air raid patrols rather often.

Dreyer was always horny, and not only for me. As the boss of an important company he virtually had free rein to do what he wanted there. There were Ukranian POWs working in his factory. All he had to do was offer to let them have a bath at his place and he'd have as many as he wanted. Word spread pretty quickly among the workers what the price was for a bath at Dreyer's. That might seem inconceivable nowadays, but during the war, when the workers didn't have an opportunity to wash themselves after a hard, dirty day's work, and since they didn't have any sex because there were no women around, well, they would go along with it.

To be honest, sexually he was not at all my type. Of course I couldn't hide that from him, and it hurt him terribly. Sure, he was good-looking, well built, and always well groomed, but for me he was just too harsh, too much man. On the other hand, he was always overcome by a typical German sentimentality. Almost every time he would start crying that he missed his little darling in Switzerland. I played along, because I basically liked him—and we needed the apartment! Besides, I did let other people come to the apartment, especially Zwi, but Dreyer didn't have to know.

Through me he got to know Mamsi. She was enchanted by him, and he trusted and grew fond of her. That was all I needed. Whenever I didn't do just what he wanted, he would run to her and complain. She knew just how to handle it. With the famous silk underwear that she gave me on June 30, 1944, for my twenty-first birthday, much to the consternation of my aunts, I was supposed to look especially seductive for Paul Dreyer. For him, I played a real stereotypically female role. I was to look erotically tempting, but by no means was I always to say yes. . . . Just the counterpart he wanted to his ardent masculinity, as a welcome and regular distraction from his lovesickness.

ALL OF AUGSBURGER STRASSE LAY IN RUINS. I sighed deeply. That meant complications, yet again. I was looking for Strunck, the escape helper. After Jizchak's successful escape, I wanted to continue to use our contact with him. We had heard from Geneva that border personnel on both sides still appeared to be cooperative.

Now Strunck's address on Augsburger Strasse didn't exist anymore. Often, in such cases, little notes would be hanging on the remains of the buildings with information about where those who were bombed out could be found. There it was; Strunck had left a note saying where he was now living.

A few days later I was standing in front of him. Nathan had given me a password, so I could identify myself: "Greetings from . . . ," and then I'd say the name of a refugee whom Strunck had helped escape to Switzerland.

The man was short; a dark, wiry, nervous type, very masculine and very curt. He didn't give an all too friendly impression, but he was very direct. "At the moment I have to take a little break, but I'll tell you how things go. We have two Wehrmacht trucks that transport munitions. Except that instead of munitions, people are lying in the crates." They were planning to cross the border into Switzerland near Singen. He seemed very sure of his plan. "But things don't happen overnight. Get me together a group of, say, twenty people. And it isn't cheap."

A shimmer of hope. How many did I know who were eagerly waiting for a chance like this! Strunck was hardened and venal. It didn't mean anything to him that he was saving Jews. He wanted thousands of marks per person.

I raced to the Löwensteins'. We hardly dared to show our enthusiasm. Six to eight weeks, Strunck had estimated. Freedom seemed to be that close.

I had to think carefully about how I wanted to approach it all. It was hard enough to choose twenty from the large number of people we would help to be the first to take a step toward freedom. Or, put another way, to be the first to take on the risk of this escape attempt. I had some priorities about whom I thought needed to get to safety more urgently than others. I didn't want to put so-called privileged *mischlings* like Arje Davidowicz on the list, something he resented terribly. Instead, I wanted to include Rudi Bernstein and Zwi and other "full Jews," as well as everyone from the inner circle of the Chug Chaluzi who was especially at risk.

The Löwensteins and I had decided that Hanna should join me at the next meeting with Strunck. I am a born matchmaker, and I was absolutely certain that Strunck would be really taken with her. He was a ladies' man, you could see that immediately, and Hans-Oskar's mother was enchanting. We thought it would be good to bring a little spark to the whole thing.

My instincts didn't betray me. He could hardly keep his eyes off her. We met several times the following week. First of all he sold us some phony identity cards. We could always use them. He somehow acquired blank IDs that he sold to us for an outrageous ten thousand marks each, but they were really good—for civilian employees at the Staaken military airfield. Strunck even had the photographs attached by specialists. Frau Löwenstein took care of that deal. We counted on the growing trust between them to keep him interested in our escape plans.

Soon he wanted the list from me. I assumed he would accept it exactly as I gave it to him, but that wasn't the case. I had put all three Löwensteins on the list. Father and son looked so Jewish that even the "mixed" marriage offered them only relative protection. And they were so involved in our work that this was enough to endanger them.

When Strunck gave me back the list, Hanna Löwenstein's name had been removed. What was that supposed to mean? Suddenly we had misgivings. We had absolutely no intention of letting families be separated. The escape was supposed to take place in three weeks. The meeting place was in the forest not far from Oranienburg, north of Berlin.

At our next meeting, Strunck had bad news. "I have to warn you. All ID cards were called in. New ones were issued four days ago, but I wasn't able to get the new forms. But don't worry, that doesn't affect the other thing." He didn't tell us how that could have happened. We held back our suspicions and told the people who were walking around with his identity cards. Aside from that, we assumed that everything else was proceeding according to plan.

Two days later Hanna Löwenstein was doing errands in Charlottenburg and ran into an old friend she had not seen in years. She was surprised that the woman was still in Berlin. The two of them rushed quickly into an inconspicuous café and started telling each other their stories. "We've been living illegally for quite some time," the other woman said, "and now six weeks ago we scraped together the rest of our money because there was a chance to escape. Imagine, in munitions crates from the Wehrmacht!" Hanna's ears pricked up. An officer who helped people escape to Switzerland? "The meeting place was in the woods near Oranienburg. On that evening, my husband and I rode there on our bicycles. That seemed safer to us. But we were late. You can't imagine, Hanna, we got there and at a distance we saw the Wehrmacht trucks driving away already! And we were standing there. Not only our money was gone, but our hopes of getting free!" Hanna didn't say a word; her head was spinning. "My husband kept his cool. 'Come on,' he said to me, 'let's follow them. They can't go that fast through the forest anyway. Maybe we can manage to keep on their trail.' So we struggled along behind them, riding as hard as we could, hoping to catch up to them at some point." The woman stopped for a moment. "And then?" Hanna Löwenstein pressed her to continue. "And then we saw how the trucks turned left—into the entrance of the Sachsenhausen concentration camp!" Hanna looked at her friend dumbfounded. All she could do was give her a hug. Four weeks later it would have been her husband and her son—and then Strunck would have tried his luck with her.

I later found out all about the thing with Strunck. He had successfully gotten a few escape transports through to Switzerland, and after that he delivered all of them to Sachsenhausen. Up to that point it had involved people who were not connected to an organization like the Hechalutz, which meant when they didn't arrive in Switzerland, there was no one to ask any mistrusting questions in Berlin. That would have been different with our group, of course.

But now we knew ahead of time. I had arranged with him that he would get his money at the Swiss border, not before, as he had originally demanded. Who knows, he might have indeed let our group escape. Or even gone with them.

He had only gotten us the forged ID cards in order to win Hanna's trust, aside from the money aspect, of course. Maybe he even arranged that the old cards got called in. In any case, at least he didn't denounce the holders of the cards, even though he knew them all by their assumed names and photographs. He was a real shady character. With heavy hearts, the Löwensteins and I decided to blow the deal off.

On July 2, 1944, I wrote to Nathan: "After we had all placed great hope in our friend Augsburg [Strunck], it has turned out that he is totally unreliable and not in a position to lead us on the way with even a trace of security." The next day, the situation had changed once again. Two refugees who had been caught in late May gave the names of both Frau Meier and Herbert Strunck. I continued the letter to Nathan, "Because of statements made, relations to the border have become useless." I asked him to send us passports that we could use to travel as far as the border. "Perhaps you can also send us addresses of people who could help us at Gvula [when crossing the border]. . . ." And so we were back at square one.

My boss, Richard Wählisch, made inspections of his construction sites regularly. He had to decide how the work should proceed. "This building is still structurally sound; it should be carefully restored," he might say; or "This should be torn down, but there are still a lot of usable items that should be removed first: stoves, doors, window frames, bathtubs."

I had to show up every now and then despite my "anemia," and one day in June we ran into each other on one of the sites. "Gypsy, come over here!" Wählisch never said "Jew." The worst thing he managed to squeak out was this absurd "Gypsy," with a friendly undertone, and that to me, a little blond boy. His workers knew he was no slavedriver. You could notice that by the fact that they didn't start obviously sweating and slaving away as soon as he'd appear.

I walked over to him. "Can you type? You wear glasses; you must be a real bookworm." Could I type? Not at all. I nodded eagerly, because I realized in a flash that I was about to get a desk job, a hundred times more pleasant than this construction-work grind. "Report to my office next Monday."

I spent the weekend with Uncle Paul and Aunt Anna. I knew they had an old typewriter, and I used it to get some practice. By Monday morning I had learned pathetically little, but more than nothing, thanks to Uncle Paul's help, which didn't limit itself to the typewriter. On Sunday, while Anna was out visiting someone, we exchanged intimacy deliberately, intentionally, for the first time. To this day I remember it with a tickling feeling in the pit of my stomach. It's amazing when you think that at the time he was pushing sixty. But he was a working man with a tough body, which stood in stark, thrilling contrast to the great tenderness he showed. He was simply my Uncle Paul, with all that history of help and attention and care.

On Monday I went to see Wählisch in his office at the Westhafen docks. The rubble from the bombed-out buildings was taken out of Berlin on huge barges, and building materials had to be shipped in, so it made sense that Wählisch would have his headquarters at the docks. A slightly downhill strip of land led to the piers, and at the bottom there were small trailers containing sparsely furnished offices to take care of loading formalities, etc.

The main office, on the other hand, was in a spacious, converted warehouse. Wählisch used a good dozen rooms there, separated from each other by window panes. The doors leading to the hall were also glassed. It was very light and gave a posh impression. The office equipment was miserable, however, as I was soon to discover. The office manager was a Jew living in a "mixed" marriage, the former director of Orenstein & Koppel, a Berlin freight car company.

I was given a little desk in this office and was supposed to write invoices. Or rather, calculations. What jobs were done for each building, how many overtime hours, how many workers, how much material, and so on. It was deadly boring. And of course I fought a constant battle with the typewriter.

After a few days Wählisch came over to me. "Not going so good yet, huh?" "Oh, Herr Wählisch, I'm really trying my best." "Hey, relax, hold your horses!" And he was gone.

On June 30 he came over again. "Well, how're things going now?" Then the wonderful office manager put in his two cents' worth: "How should things be going, Herr Wählisch? The boy's fingers are ruined from the work on the site. They have to get used to the new job. Besides, today is the kid's birthday." Why does he have to tell him that, I thought. "Oh yeah?" Wählisch responded, smiling, and added, "Well, let's see. I'll come by again later."

Two hours later, he really did come by again. "Come on, put on your jacket!" My mother had made me a white jacket that I was wearing for the first time that day. Wählisch took me to Haus Vaterland at Potsdamer Platz. It was a huge building with a café on the ground level and banquet halls and conference rooms above. Each floor was named for a different region. At that time, only the café was still open to the public.

He ordered me an ice cream. I was thinking the whole time, Why is he doing this? I couldn't figure out what his motive could be. I had already met his wife, a hideous old bag, and their almost grown-up daughter. A common Berlin working-class family; I didn't like them.

But he looked at me sideways with a friendly expression and patted me on the shoulder in a very lighthearted way. "A nice way to celebrate your birthday, huh?" Slowly it all started to click. This important man, who constantly had appointments and was always racing from one construction site to the next and then back to the office, did not have any time to relax and spend an hour with me in a café. It must mean he was more than just well-meaning. He must take me, the little Jewish guy, seriously. I decided to bet the whole wad at once.

"No, actually, it's not such a great day for me," I responded in a despondent tone. "Why not?" Wählisch was half concerned and half indignant that his generosity evidently hadn't pleased me enough.

"I'm going to have to stop working soon." "What? But you can't! What are you talking about?" I had to take advantage of every chance I saw to get help. "You know, I help some guys who are living illegally, and soon I'm going to go underground as well." So now it was out. How would he react? But what did I have to lose anyway? He wouldn't have me arrested right there on the spot. Not him. And I really could disappear out of his life as soon as we said goodbye. I could only win.

He looked at me with an expression I could only describe as loving. "Gee, kid, that must be tough. But maybe things could be easier." I was listening. "Well," he added, "maybe I could help you guys." Now I was speechless. I didn't expect him to go that far. I mean, he could let us use whole buildings if he wanted to. I was all excited.

The first suggestion he made was something we continued to take advantage of to the end. He became very businesslike, as though he had prepared himself for our conversation, and immediately stopped speaking with the unrefined Berlin accent. "At the Westhafen docks, you know? Of the four loading piers, only three are in use. The fourth is for emergencies and special cases, but I always know a little ahead of time. Come on, I'll give you a key for the corresponding trailer." The grounds were neither fenced in nor guarded—who would steal rubble? Only the trailers were locked. And then he got really soft and personal again, and his accent returned: "And I'll always leave you guys something to eat."

Now, that was a phenomenal birthday present. Not only did I get a new place to stay, but I also had virtually full freedom of movement. We arranged that Wählisch would continue to keep me on the books, although I never worked there a single day once we got things settled. That actually led to problems after the war. In terms of government compensation for persecutees, no one believed at first that I had lived illegally, since I was meticulously listed in Wählisch's books day by day, and so health insurance and pension plan were paid for me.

On the day after my birthday, we went together to Westhafen after work and inspected the trailer. "Yeah, well," he said pragmatically, "it'll need some work. I'll bring you a mattress so you won't all have to sleep on the wooden bench." My retort was just as practical: "Starting day after tomorrow I'm sick. Anemia. I told them at the company already."

From then on there really was always something in the trailer to eat, coffee to drink, even luxury items. When he came back from a business trip to Italy once, there was so much stuff we had to arrange a car to smuggle it all out without being noticed!

In the course of the final war years, about ten illegals stayed in the trailer. Many of our secret hiding places belonged to money-hungry, unfriendly people who by no means felt or acted like hosts. The sleeping accommodations were usually filthy and uncomfortable, and on top of that, they made a pile of money off us. Our trailer, in contrast, was pure luxury. Wählisch even left clean linens whenever he was there! That alone must have been great for the boys, to have a place to totally relax that was clean and friendly.

Of course the boss wanted something in return; I already got the idea when we were eating the ice cream. He wanted me. I wasn't totally uninterested. He was a construction-worker type with some signs of a paunch, but he was muscular. And on that day in the café I had already noticed that he had something to offer in his pants. He was wearing light gabardine slacks that brought out his anatomy nicely.

We would arrange our meetings through notes. I would write when I planned to come to the trailer, and he would make "control rounds" outside. Then the boss would disappear into one of the trailers . . . to make some coffee! No one kept tabs very closely. I wasn't supposed to call him on the phone, and I never did.

In our fifteen or twenty meetings I had the feeling it was his way of putting everything aside for a few moments—the responsibility of the company, the war, the dismal times we were living in. He could do or not do whatever he wanted, far removed from reality, and on top of that he was doing something good for those of us he was helping. For him it was a combination of moral action, his own desires, and the appeasement of his feelings of guilt. We never talked politics. He was well aware that that would have been problematic. One single time a sentence slipped out that said it all: "Man, I'm getting rich off your backs."

WHEN I SAID GOODBYE to Helga Ammann, my pigskin briefcase was once again full of cash, and I was on my way to Fritz Löwenstein. The humid July swelter was baking the city, and I was sweating in my far too elegant clothing, which I had worn for Helga's sake. This time we had met for lunch in the Zigeunerkeller, the Gypsy Cellar, on Kurfürstendamm, which was a rarity.

I hadn't gone a hundred steps before the sirens started sounding. People were yelling out information they had heard on the radio. "They're flying in en masse! But they're only as far as Magdeburg." Everyone was running like crazy. I had gotten to the corner of Joachimstaler Strasse when I decided to go back to the Zigeunerkeller, which was an authorized air raid shelter.

Then I noticed a young man across the street who was incredibly well dressed. You didn't see that very often. Young men who were not on the front definitely did not have nice clothing to wear. He looked a bit older, maybe because of the hat. But as soon as our eyes met, I realized immediately that I knew him.

The last time I had seen him was thirteen years ago, at elementary school in Weissensee. He was one of my two "big friends," the Gypsy brothers!

I walked over to him and said, "Aren't you Herzberg?!" His response: "You must be the blond kid from my class!" What a reunion!

We smiled. Then I came back to the present. "It's an air raid. We have to get out of here. I'm going to the Zigeunerkeller." He put his arm around me and came along. It was totally natural, like two soldiers on leave seeing each other again for the first time. The Zigeunerkeller was almost empty. The musician who worked there didn't have to play that afternoon, and he joined us. Herzberg knew him.

Then he told me how fate had treated him. He had a permit to play as a violinist in the Berlin Philharmonic, albeit as a foreigner (though he was born in Berlin); it was still valid even though the Philharmonic had already closed. His work and residence permit was still good for another few weeks. The other man, Dajos Béla, head of the famous Jazz Symphony Orchestra, lived totally legally in Berlin.

Herzberg asked Béla if he had anything; he meant food, of course. They took care of their black market deals through the Zigeunerkeller. Béla didn't have anything but told him he would the next day. Spontaneously, I said I would join them. But for now, I had to get to the Löwensteins'.

After dropping off the money, I went with Hans-Oskar to the movies. We had made the date quite a while before, and luckily the air raid was over. We went to the matinee showing at the Filmbühne Wien. Back then it was a huge, plush cinema with a Wurlitzer organ. *Die Frau meiner Träume* (The Woman of My Dreams), starring Marika Rökk, was an entertaining, schmaltzy film with dancing and singing. I enjoyed the kitsch as a welcome distraction. Besides that, I liked how our knees would touch in the dark and our fingers would wander. . . .

When we walked out onto the street after the movie there were soldiers marching, military trucks with machine guns rolling down Kurfürstendamm, something indecipherable being called out through a megaphone. The pedestrians didn't really know what was happening, but there were rumors about the Führer having been assassinated. We ran as fast as we could to the Löwensteins'.

That was July 20, 1944, and there were contradictory reports on the radio. Before long, however, we heard the disappointing news that Hitler was still alive. We didn't even have time to paint ourselves a picture of what might've happened if he were dead—if the war would have been over, what would happen with the concentration camps, with the Jews, with us, the illegals. . . . The bubble had burst before we could even appreciate its enticing shimmer.

Everything continued as before. Although my parents had since returned to their apartment on Prenzlauer Strasse, I stayed in my "headquarters"; that was safest for all of us. In addition to Elly Peipe's apartment in the Wedding district and Wählisch's trailer at the Westhafen docks, I also had a few other bases where I could spend a night. For example, I had arranged with my aunts and uncles that whenever I was absolutely wasted, I could go to them for twenty-four hours and unwind: eat, bathe, sleep, like on an oasis. The few times I took advantage of this paradise, it helped me collect myself and my thoughts, abate my fears, replenish my strength, and reassure myself of my goals.

Then there was also Giovanni, my Italian; we still got together sporadically. My assumed name, Günther Kaplan, was on the visitors' list at his camp on Prenzlauer Allee, so I could go there whenever I wanted. Giovanni would arrange for me to eat there, and then we'd share his bed for the night.

It was only due to this far-reaching network of friends, acquaintances, helpers, suppliers, hiding places, and contacts that I was able to withstand the psychological pressures connected with living illegally. My situation was fundamentally different from that of others living underground in one regard. They were often in one hiding place for a long time, having to remain as invisible as possible for as long as possible, until they were forced to move on to a new hiding place. In contrast, I was constantly on the move, outdoors, in the city, among people. That resembled freedom more than the "normal" illegal existence, but it also meant a lot more responsibility and a much greater risk. That was the only way I was able not to lose sight of the meaning of life in these insane times.

In September 1944 I received a message from the Wallach brothers by way of a nurse at the Jewish Hospital at Schulstrasse 78: "All five of us are here!" Starting in March 1944 the assembly camp was transferred little by little from Grosse Hamburger Strasse to the Jewish Hospital in the Wedding district. They didn't need so much space anymore, since fewer and fewer people were being deported, or rather, were still around to be deported. But transports were definitely still taking place, and five of the people I was taking care of were in the assembly camp!

It gave me an incredible start. That meant I had failed. Our agreement about what to do in an emergency hadn't worked. What had happened?

The Wallachs were part of a small group of remaining *chaverim* from the former *hachsharot* in the environs of Berlin. In April 1943 the last of these work camps had already been closed. The "full Jews," such as Karla Wagenberg, were deported to Auschwitz; the *mischlings* were scattered throughout Brandenburg to do slave labor in agriculture and forestry. Their future seemed uncertain.

I had been writing letters to five of them. There were the three Wallach brothers: Alfred (Amnon), Erich (Mordechai), and Kurt. Their Jewish father had been deported, but they weren't living with their Christian mother either, which would have made them a little safer. There was also a girl named Rita (Shoshanna) Fränkel, whose Christian father ran a restaurant in the Rhineland, but he hadn't done much to help her, which is why she was in great risk of getting sent to the "milder" concentration camp, Theresienstadt. And the fifth was Paul Safirstein, another *mischling* with unclear status, who on top of everything wasn't very strong because he suffered from asthma.

Since the summer of 1943 they had been in the forestry work camp in Jacobsdorf working for a farmer. At that time, farmers could officially pick up boys and girls from the work camps to help with the harvest if all their farm hands were fighting on the front lines. Early in summer 1944 we agreed I should go to Jacobsdorf to discuss their uncertain situation.

Making the trip from the center of Berlin to Jacobsdorf, which is practically at the gates of Frankfurt on the Oder, about fifty miles away, was a real odyssey. I left early one Sunday morning and took the S-Bahn to the suburb of Erkner, then transferred to a small train that went as far as a tiny village called Pillgram, really at the end of the world. One other man got out with me, and that was it. Basically, the train station was in the middle of nowhere; there was only countryside around.

The man asked me, "Where do you want to go?" "To Jacobsdorf." He laughed. "You can't make it on foot. If you start now, it'll be too late for you to get back in time. You wouldn't make the last train to Berlin. And especially on a Sunday, forget it." I was at a loss. Then he said, "Come on. I have a bicycle, and I'm going in the same direction."

I had never sat on a bicycle in my life. It was quite an adventure. To make things worse, the forest started right there, so there were bumpy paths, tree roots, stones, everything the heart desired. By the time we arrived I was dripping with sweat.

I saw the five of them for the first time at the farmer's. My journey to the countryside aroused wistful recollections of the time I spent at Skaby. Of the many energetic young Zionists, only a handful remained, and Palestine had faded to a mere chimera. I had actually come to talk the small group into trying to escape. But Mordechai, with whom I could talk about it best because he had exchanged letters with Nathan, thought they were safe in Jacobsdorf at least until fall, since the farmer needed them for the harvest.

We agreed that if, counter to all expectations, they were threatened with a transport sooner, they would go into hiding and contact me in Berlin. Then Mordechai rode me to the station on his bicycle, so I made the train back to Berlin.

Three months later, the emergency had happened. And it was even worse. My charges were already interned.

The Jewish Hospital on Schulstrasse was a strange place in Berlin during the final years of the war. It had gradually acquired four different functions: In addition to normal hospital operations, it served as a military hospital for soldiers injured on the front lines. In the basement were the detention and jail cells of the assembly camp. On the upper floors, numerous so-called protected Jews (according to Göring: "I decide who is a Jew!") lived in the hospital rooms. Altogether, supposedly almost a thousand of them had lived there in the course of the war. In June 1943 the Jewish Hospital also housed the New Reich Association, the successor to the Reich Association of Jews. It was supposed to be the last central Jewish institution in a state that was *judenrein*. You could find specialists there, for example, who worked together with the Reich Economics Office. A few people in one office did work that could be considered a kind of final "Jewish Community representation" (cooperating with the Gestapo). There were also Jews or *mischlings* who had passports from neutral countries, some thanks to Nathan Schwalb. They were a colorful mixture, and not all of them were strictly aboveboard—like the former Jewish secretary in the Soviet embassy in Berlin, or the two men who designed economic plans for the government in Budapest, who were picked up by the Gestapo every morning in a Mercedes and brought back every evening.

The prisoners in the assembly camp were put in huge basement rooms with bars on the doors and windows, in the former pathology department of the hospital underneath a pavilionlike extension. There was a separate entrance onto Schulstrasse. But the assembly camp itself was separated from the rest of the hospital by barbed wire.

I met the nurse who had sent me the message from the Wallachs. Her name was Lea Jacob, and she worked in the "Jewish section." A sweet little dumpling. She took care of Paul Safirstein, who needed regular injections for his asthma, and a romance soon developed between the two.

Lea warned me, "Gad, the five of them have to get out of here. There are still transports taking place. A whole bunch of people were deported just a few weeks ago." We made a plan.

The Wallachs had to do slave labor clearing up rubble from bombardments. Lea knew that the address of the site was Französische Strasse.

Shoshanna Fränkel wasn't put to work, but she was depressed and ill. Lea said, "I'll issue a request form for her saying she needs orthopedic shoes. She can get away from the marshal while she's at the shoemaker's." And Paul Safirstein was on Lea's ward anyway. She could arrange his escape herself.

We decided that the Wallachs should make their getaway on the same day as Paul at exactly 12:30 P.M. and meet at my apartment. It wasn't all that difficult to escape from a construction site. All the boys had to do was tell the foreman that they had to take a pee. In the middle of ruins, who's going to keep tabs on who disappears behind which pile of rubble to relieve themselves?

It wasn't all that easy for Kurt, the youngest, even though his job was a very simple one. He stood at the side of the road and stacked bricks that the others brought him. All he had to do was step behind the pile and run across the street. But that dreamer didn't manage to get it together until the very last moment.

The alarm sounded as soon as someone noticed that the boys had disappeared. At the very latest, it had to have become obvious to the Gestapo at that point that an organized group was behind the escape.

The guys showed up at my apartment on Utrechter Strasse one after another, panting and puffing. Shoshanna had been too afraid to run away. That evening Lea joined us as well. She and Paul Safirstein celebrated their success in my bed, so enthusiastically that the pictures almost fell off the walls. They later married in the United States, had a son, and were happy together until Paul's death.

Two days later, Paul Dreyer showed up at my place, without advance notice as usual and looking forward to having a little fun. Instead of just me he found five boys there: The two older Wallachs were lying on the double bed with Zwi, and little Kurt was on the couch. Lea had already taken Paul Safirstein with her to find safe lodgings for him.

I was scared to death and thought all hell would break loose. But then he showed his queenish side. Instead of having a fit, he squealed enthusiastically, "Oh! Oh! So many pretty boys!"

I was able to convince him that no orgy was taking place, and in any case none that he would be welcome to join. Without a complaint, he turned and left. All in all Paul Dreyer was a good person.

It was not until during this time that I really got to know little Kurt, whom everyone called Mousey. He was neither little nor mousey at all but rather tall, and aside from that he wasn't all that young; he was seventeen. But he was terribly dependent. Kurt could only fall asleep if he rolled up into a ball and put a corner of his "blankey" in his mouth. During air raids he would get really frightened. He would never go into an air raid shelter; instead he would crawl underneath his bed.

It seemed as though Kurt might turn into one big burden. Zwi looked at it pragmatically: "It will be hard to protect him. But if they get him, they'll get us. Just don't tell him too much." His brothers were more clever and optimistic: "Oh, we'll manage okay; they won't get us." They were great sports.

It was definitely somewhat foolish to think four or five of us could stay in this one-room ground-floor apartment. It couldn't have been more obvious. We never went to the air raid shelter in the building, since as a group we definitely looked too Jewish. This juggling act was not a long-term solution.

It was no secret to our guests that Zwi and I had sex together. Even little Kurt, who was sad, scared, and couldn't sleep, knew what was going on. He simply needed affection and closeness. I got to be fond of him and gave him some of that closeness—of course, not when Zwi happened to be around.

Kurt had grown out of all his clothes, but he never said anything. He wore a one-piece combination—nowadays you call it a bodysuit—but it was the size for a fourteen-year-old. And of course he hadn't changed his clothes in ages. His whole bottom was chafed from wearing this too-small, unwashed piece of clothing.

I took our dirty washing to Aunt Frieda at regular intervals; at least I could arrange that much. Then the four of us discussed this bodysuit. "Mousey, you can't wear it anymore," said Amnon, "you gotta take it off." "Why? Do I stink?" asked Kurt. We all stank. We lived in very close quarters, always on the go. We only had cold water; of course, we couldn't wash ourselves decently. Mousey was incredibly embarrassed when he finally took the thing off. Life in the underground was simply not a very sophisticated matter.

STICKS OF BOMBS STARTED FALLING on the city the same month. They were huge bombs in close succession dropped along a street. Ten or twelve bombs detonated one after another, and the buildings were lifted from underneath, collapsing like a row of dominos. The row of dominos on Utrechter Strasse ended with our next-door neighbors. The outer wall of our apartment was blown in slightly, but it didn't collapse. Through a crack you could see outside. Now I had to hurry up and find somewhere else for the guys to stay.

It was just about impossible to find a place for all three of them together.

Mousey alone was more than enough for any "host." For him, I thought of a woman from our Communist connections who had an apartment on the outskirts of the city. She let us put people up there sometimes, since she needed the money. She rejected us, like almost everyone who had party or ideological ties. Their strange argument went like this: "You're only opposed to the Nazis because you want to survive, not because of political convictions." These people insisted on the proper ideological attitudes. But in the end the woman needed money and finally decided to take Mousey off my hands.

Eight days later he was back at my door, with a note from her. It said, "The kid is impossible. That just won't do. He doesn't help with anything. I'm keeping the money since I did my best, but he has to go." She was at her wit's end. So now his brothers would have to figure out what to do with him.

With regard to the other two brothers, I had turned to Frau Szimke. I visited her regularly anyway, in order to get food supplies and because she sometimes received packages for us from Switzerland: shoes, clothing, and food. I had to use utmost diplomatic politeness to collect them, or else she would've kept them all herself, or at least taken charge of distributing the stuff. That September I scored again.

"Oh, that was dropped off here for you," she chirped innocently, as I was already standing in front of a plastic bag with a Zurich address on it. I laughed to myself. "Oh, what a coincidence that I happened to come by," I said. "Saves you the trouble of having to notify me."

She didn't notice my smugness. I continued, "But I also have another question. I have to find a place for two guys to stay. It's pretty urgent. Know of anything?"

Since she had already temporarily housed Jizchak and Zwi, I had hoped she'd find room for the Wallachs as well. She hesitated a moment before giving me an indirect answer. "Remember the woman who was here recently to buy coffee, like you were? She's in the oldest profession in the world, not that it matters. Anyway, I hinted something to her about you boys. She had already gotten wind of it, and I think she'd like to help you."

I was astounded. "How does she know anything?"

"She can tell you herself. Wait just a minute. Could be that she'll be right over."

"Could be"? She had to be kidding. I had the feeling the lady was waiting in the wings. Szimke disappeared, and five minutes later I was standing there with Fräulein Schmidt.

The group of prostitutes that she was part of used the Mexiko Bar as their base. It was at the corner of Prenzlauer Strasse and Alexanderplatz, one of the seediest meeting places in the city. She would take her johns "up to her room," for example, to Szimke's, a block away.

Fräulein Schmidt didn't beat around the bush. "So I'll tell you the story from the very beginning. I work here at Alexanderplatz, around the corner. But I usually do business with somewhat more refined gentlemen." I didn't find that very probable, but her explanation was good. She said mysteriously, "Because I'm of better standing."

Not until much later did I find out that she really did come from an aristocratic family. On that day I simply smiled politely. Something like reminiscence or nostalgia seemed to flash by her before she continued. "About four weeks ago they told the other girls and me to come to the Wehrmacht, to the commando for support of the troops. A doctor examined us, and then most of my colleagues were sent to the front lines for, well, to support the troops. I wasn't among them, and I asked the duty officer: 'So what's with me? You haven't told me what to do.' 'Oh,' he said, 'you're healthy. You can go home.' 'What?' I said, 'I'm not being sent to the front with the others?' 'No, not you,' he said, 'you're too old.' Then I blew up. 'Well, little man,' I said, 'day before yesterday I was good enough for your colonel. Now I'm too old for your simple soldiers?' He wasn't impressed. Just because I'm over forty. Then I was standing outside, and I said to myself: 'Not with me, they don't do that. They are dead to me now.' And that's why we're here talking today. Frau Szimke just told me about your problem." She took a deep breath. "Your two guys can stay here in my room. I have other options. But I'll tell you one thing right now, so you don't get any funny ideas. I won't touch either of them. They'll have it good with me."

I was moved. I understood immediately that the humiliation she had experienced made her into a highly motivated comrade-in-arms. I could use that kind of help.

Fräulein Schmidt was the plump, matronly type, mid-forties, somewhat worn out, with a puffy face. She had a bleached blond permanent that they used to call a "baker's wife" hairdo. She didn't smoke, didn't seem common or vulgar, and wore little makeup, though she did pluck her eyebrows. All in all she looked like your basic middle-class housewife. That must have had a calming effect on soldiers home on leave.

I took an immediate liking to her, not only because she seemed pleasant from the start. There was another reason, one she knew nothing about. It had something to do with a little episode from 1942 that occurred to me while I was talking to her.

My aunts had gotten some fabric for us so my mother could sew a dress for Miriam for her birthday. It was a light, pretty summer dress with polka dots and puffed sleeves. Everyone was pleased, and Miriam wore it every

Sunday. But after a few weeks, she stormed home angry. My mother was upset. "What happened, dear?" "Oh, nothing. It's just that I can't wear the dress anymore." "Why not? Is it too tight?" "No," Miriam snarled, and then she burst into tears. "Down there at the corner, the lady with the handbag that's always standing there, she's wearing exactly the same dress, even with the same dumb puffed sleeves!" And what was Fräulein Schmidt wearing, two years later at Frau Szimke's? Polka dots and puffed sleeves! I believe in coincidences.

In the fall of 1944, a second courier came from Nathan Schwalb, a man who called himself Axel Rudolph, among other assumed names, including Count Kronenburg. Rudolph was a sophisticated, good-looking, adventuresome type, whose secret activities were not limited to courier services in Berlin. He also worked for the British secret service. He had connections all over. He'd bring me Roth-Händle cigarettes, cigars, whatever I needed. If I needed special, elegant clothing, he'd get it from Baden-Baden. On top of that, he had various lovers and confidantes in various cities.

Rudolph had also developed good contacts around the German-Swiss border. Now new escape options were supposed to be tested, and he offered to personally accompany one refugee—my sister, Miriam—to the unpatrolled border near Radolfzell. From there she was to proceed on foot into Switzerland. At that time she had a forged Post Office ID card but no other convincing papers. Rudolph assured us that nothing could go wrong; after all, he would be with her.

During the trip he immediately started making moves on Miriam. That explains why he wanted to accompany only one refugee, namely her. When she resisted his advances, he literally abandoned her along the way.

But she basically knew what she had to do without him. Nathan had explained everything in a letter. The decisive words, once again, were written in Hebrew, including one little word that referred to the final destination of her journey. It was *Meches,* which means "customs station." I had decoded the letter for Miriam, but I didn't know that word. Not wanting to admit my shortcoming, I improvised. Some station, maybe a railroad station? A town called Mecheln?

From the hotel, Miriam was supposed to take a path through the forest, continuing straight ahead until she reached *Meches.* There she would be met by Swiss border guards. But at some point the path turned, and the one that continued straight ahead didn't seem like the main path. Instead of reaching Switzerland, Miriam ended up within sight of a group of German soldiers, whom she barely managed to avoid.

It must have been terrible for the poor girl, to be so close and yet not find the window to freedom! All that was left was to give up and return to Berlin. What else could she have done? On the return trip she had to make it through all the passport controls on the train by herself. She was lucky; no one discovered that her papers were forged. We were absolutely devastated, because we thought the contact with Nathan had been broken off, since she didn't run into any of the people who had been waiting for her.

It was especially unpleasant for me, since Nathan had expressed in a few previous letters his impatience and disappointment that we were not organizing any escape attempts although appropriate arrangements had been made at the border. I tried to explain what had gone wrong with Miriam's escape and make it clear to him how little leeway we had in Berlin.

Believe me, Nathan, we aren't cowards. Every single step we make is being followed and every knock at the door could mean our end, yet we continue despite everything and even, when necessary, help the chaverim to Yetziah [rescue] directly out of the hands of the Mishtara [Gestapo] [I'm referring to the escape of the Wallachs], in order to make it possible for them too to have Yetziah and reach you. All of this should be evidence enough of our intrepidity and courage. . . .

In October 1944 I was referred to Otto Ullstein in one of the letters from Switzerland. He was one of the last of the great Ullstein publishing dynasty in Berlin, a great-nephew of the elder Ullstein. He lived in the Charlottenburg district, in the west, and I was supposed to check in on him and bring greetings from a relative who had emigrated. That was all the information I had when I set off to visit him.

An elderly woman opened the door for me. I said, "I am here from Zurich and have greetings to deliver." I mentioned the name of the relative. Of course I was wearing my fancy suit. The woman looked at me for a moment, then whispered, "One moment, please," and disappeared into the apartment.

After a while I could hear a deep voice in the background: "Well, why not? Let him in." The man, sitting in a small room in the back, had a body that resembled a whale. His clothing must have been custom-made, and later I heard that the chairs he sat on were also produced specially for him. He only moved back and forth between bed, chair, and bathroom; other than that, the elderly woman took care of all his needs.

Ullstein tried to "hibernate" and totally ignore what was going on in the outside world. Although he had had the chance to emigrate, his state of health was such that he could not have boarded a train, plane, or ship. He obviously had enough money, and his accommodations appeared secure. Everything was fine. He exuded a correspondingly good mood. Feel free to come again; give my regards as well. "Do you need anything?" I added,

"Don't hesitate to say something." Coffee was the only thing he could think of.

Four weeks later I went by again, coffee in hand. The woman stood at the door and said, "Oh, it's better if you don't come in. I'll come down to the entrance." Was something the matter upstairs? It didn't sound like a Gestapo trap.

When she was downstairs standing before me, I asked with concern what the matter was. "Herr Kaplan, he doesn't want to go on anymore. He's going to commit suicide." "Nonsense, the war'll be over soon," I said. "No, it has already lasted a lot longer than he estimated." I didn't understand a word. "He's almost out of cigars!"

This man had at some point calculated how long the war might last in order to horde enough of his favorite cigars so he could have one a day. He had filled his entire clothes closet with them, with a humidity gauge and a humidifier in the room so they wouldn't dry out. And now he had only two boxes left, since he had miscalculated, and he wanted to kill himself before the dreaded withdrawal set in.

To be quite honest, things like that really made me angry. There were people fighting for their naked survival, against persecution and starvation, and here's this fatso in his Charlottenburg apartment living the good life and he wants to take his life because his Havanas threaten to run out!

"Herr Kaplan, he is going to jump out the window!" the woman yammered. "He won't jump anywhere," I retorted dryly. "He wouldn't make it onto the window sill."

But Nathan did tell me to look after the gentleman. So, where would I get Havana cigars in October 1944? I turned to Axel Rudolph. "Oh, come on, boy," he laughed, "they don't have to be the same brand. I'll get good cigars; he'll have to be happy with that." Rudolph got me ten boxes of cigars, which would get Ullstein through the next nine months.

Well, dearest Nathan, all my dear friends,

Once again I want to assure you that we are doing everything in our power, as little as that is, since after what has been happening the last few weeks, we are very much aware of what we have to expect.

Help us!! We are otherwise rather helpless. Rest assured that we will not disappoint you. It is impossible for us to tell you about all the individual problems, but they are massive. Since I expect your answer directly, I send my greetings to you, dear Schwalby, and all the friends and especially Eretzia [Eretz Israel], and we are hoping as never before!

You are always in our thoughts!

Warm regards. Hope to hear from you and see you soon.

Yours, Gad

A call for help from Berlin. One of the many letters to Nathan Schwalb in Geneva. January 1945.

6

WHEN TOLD ALL AT ONCE LIKE THIS, living illegally sounds, on the one hand, like a chain of anecdotes and, on the other hand, like an inestimable mass of activities and jobs all to be done at once. And that is exactly what it was really like. My days were as full of appointments as a manager's calendar.

Take a normal day in November 1944. I lived in Elly Peipe's apartment on Utrechter Strasse. The nearest stop on streetcar line 8 was on Seestrasse. It ran up and down all over the city, and usually it was with the 8-car that I started my day.

The streetcar was always crowded. Service was constantly being suspended, on bus lines too, due to damaged sections of track or road. I liked to stand in a corner, just when the car was getting full. The pushing and squeezing often allowed for exciting moments of physical contact with strangers.

On this particular morning, my first stop was at Mamsi's on Binzstrasse in the Pankow district. We got together often, since she was part of my inner circle. I discussed everything with her—from food acquisition to questions of lodgings and the most recent plans for escape.

Mamsi was usually at home. Her official job now was to alter and repair uniforms of soldiers who had been killed. But today she wasn't there. Her mother came to the door. "These clothes stink terribly," the older woman complained. "Ruthy couldn't take it anymore, and since the weather is so wonderful, she took it all with her and went to the park." And that's where I found her. A pile to her left and a pile to her right. In the middle sat Mamsi, concentrating hard behind her large glasses. Lips pursed, nose slightly wrinkled, she was sewing with a nimble hand.

140

I teased her a bit. There really was a pretty nauseating smell of corpses emanating from the clothes. But there were worse jobs. "How do things look for meat?" I asked in a low voice. She had good connections to a butcher named Bruno who got us some horsemeat every now and again. "Not so famous at the moment, Bobby," she answered, using her pet name for me. "He said he'll let me know. But my mother can get some flour. Come back the day after tomorrow with some people who can carry it away." She couldn't say anything about the price; that depended on her mother's finesse at making the deal. I was about to leave, but she held me back: "I have to tell you one thing, though, Bobby. I was talking to Paul yesterday, and he isn't at all happy with you!"

That was all I needed. Paul Dreyer ran to her with all his worries and problems, at least when they involved me. A few days before he had come by "to check on things," as he put it. He came once a week, as agreed upon. That was sometimes a real pain in the neck. And recently I hadn't given him the sex he came for—because I had an appointment—and Dreyer hampered my timetable in a big way. So, okay, I might have been a little short with him, but what was I anyway, his concubine, ready and willing at the snap of his fingers? Mamsi tried to convince me that Dreyer's help was so important for all of us, and he was, after all, such a charming man. . . . Maybe she was right.

The next place I had to go was Richard Wählisch's office on Landsberger Allee. A few weeks before, his building at the docks had been so badly damaged by bombs that the whole business had been moved.

The new grounds had a row of single-story barracks around a large courtyard where his fleet of vehicles was standing. The office rooms in the barracks were accessed by outdoor stairways and walkways. The whole thing looked far less respectable and attractive than the complex at Westhafen.

I asked my way through to his rooms. There I saw not only other workers with whom I had gotten along well, such as the office manager, but also Wählisch's executive secretary, who never liked me. She told me snippily that Herr Wählisch was down in the courtyard giving instructions to his drivers, I should know after all how busy he is. . . .

I found him in a corner of the courtyard surrounded by a group of drivers. He was standing there in his elegant Italian suit, yet he looked like one of them, industrious and clumsy at the same time. When he saw me, he signaled that I should wait.

A little while later we were sitting together against the wall on a thick board propped between two sawhorses. He was taking his lunch break, eating a sandwich while talking with me. Such a semipublic conversation was generally safer than one upstairs in his barracks, with the old bag in the next room.

"Rudi Bernstein has to give up his hiding place temporarily, because the nephew of the woman hiding him is coming home on leave," I reported, "so I wanted to give him the trailer." We hadn't used the hideout for a few weeks, and there was some preparation to do.

Wählisch always liked to take care of several things at once. Today was no different. "How long will your friend need the trailer? A few days? Good, he can come by tomorrow. I'll take care of everything. And next week, after he's gone, we can meet there. I brought you some things from Italy. Make sure you have enough money and enough time."

After all, he was also a businessman. I marked the rendezvous with Italian delicacies in my mental calendar, and we said goodbye with a firm handshake and conspiratorial grins.

I had enough money with me, about five thousand marks; they were meant not for Wählisch but for one of my food sources—Kindler, a retired police officer. That's what the sign on his door said; one could hardly come up with a better cover for black market trading.

The second time I was there, a few months earlier, I had already gotten quite a scare. A soldier was standing in the living room as I walked in. "Don't worry, Günther," the older man said to me, "that's my son Helmut." Helmut Kindler grew up to be the well-known publisher. He knew that his father traded in black market goods and helped Jews as well. Sometimes Helmut even helped out running errands; no one suspected someone wearing a uniform.

This time there was someone else there. It wasn't my turn yet. Ahead of me were two elderly women whom Kindler had served, and there was a problem of some sort.

"Herr Kindler, we urgently need the food. Otherwise the boy will starve us to death!"

"But you have to understand me too, ladies. I have to pay good money for the food also. I can't just give it away to you!"

I decided to get involved. I already had an idea what it was about, and I was right. The two women were hiding a Jew in their summer bungalow. Without further ado I paid their bill. After all, isn't that what Nathan sent me the money for?

Later I started directly supplying the Jew they were hiding. It was Hans Rosenthal, who later became a famous TV game show host. After the war he once pulled me aside and said: "It's all your fault!" I didn't know what he was talking about. "I hate bacon! The smell alone makes me sick!" Then

I remembered. That winter I had gotten him a good bacon rind because it had a lot of calories. He had to hang out in the bungalow forcing down that bacon for weeks; he had some dry bread too, but that was all. It must have been revolting—but he survived.

On that day in November things went quickly at Kindler's; he had made his deliveries a few days earlier, and now he just needed to get his money. "I'll come by again next week," I said as I left, as always.

Meanwhile, it was early afternoon. I had a late appointment with Fritz Löwenstein. I had kept some free time in between especially so I could go "home." On the way to western Berlin, I had to go by Alexanderplatz, so I stopped off at Frau Szimke's to check on Amnon and Mordechai Wallach, who were staying in Fräulein Schmidt's "girl's room."

The streetcar I took was in terrible condition. Almost all the windows were broken, and the wind whistled through the car. Sometimes everyone would have to get out because the tracks were damaged. Then we'd have to walk a few blocks to catch another tram along the same line to continue along the route. Today we made it without any interruptions. The closer we got to the city center, the greater the extent of bomb damage.

I tried to see the increasing destruction of my city from a purely practical perspective. We illegals faced the air raids with mixed feelings. On one hand, we were in just as much danger and suffered as much from the bombs as everyone else; on the other hand, however, we were happy about anything the Allied forces were doing to hurt the Nazis.

I mostly noticed changes within my network. If I saw a destroyed building where one of our suppliers had lived or where someone had been in hiding, then all I could think was, Oh no, where can I find them, if they are even still alive!

There was nothing new at Else Szimke's. Mordechai and his brother were in good spirits. They were among my least problematic cases anyway; they were always cheerful and optimistic. Fräulein Schmidt was out and about, and I didn't have any business to do with Szimke herself today.

I had arranged to meet my mother two blocks from our home on Prenzlauer Strasse. I had cigarettes for my father and wanted to know if there was anything up.

My mother looked tired and weary, but she tried to hide it as best she could. We greeted each other with a quick hug. I asked about my father while handing her the cigarettes. And Nathan Schwalb had written another letter!

I was always very excited to get mail from him. In this letter he told me that a courier would be coming. I noted in my head: Contact Helga, tell Löwenstein.

While we were talking, my mother and I continued walking past the city hall, up to the palace. Along the way I ate the sandwiches she had brought me. That was typical; I never had to worry about meals. I always got something to eat somewhere, and I never went hungry. Then the warning siren sounded, and we looked around to see where the closest air raid shelter was. Usually, in such cases you just had to follow the crowd.

We hadn't gone very far when she giggled, a little embarrassed, and said, "Son, you can't imagine how bad I have to go to the toilet!" We were in the middle of the city, and people were rushing helter-skelter. What should she do? She was so agitated anyway and . . . it started trickling down her legs. So she had to go into the air raid shelter with wet clothes. Was she humiliated? She laughed! What else was there for her to do? She was never one to make a fuss.

Luckily it didn't take very long until the all-clear signal came. I didn't think about the time until we were back out on the street. It was already six o'clock! I had to be at the Löwensteins' at seven, and it wasn't clear whether I could make it there in an hour.

I decided to take the U-Bahn. Usually I would take the S-Bahn from Alexanderplatz to Charlottenburg, but the trains often ended up stopping forever between stations. . . .

The city was overflowing with people carrying suitcases and more suitcases. Some had been bombed out; others were refugees who had just arrived or people from the city on their way to relatives in the countryside; or else everyone was on the way to the air raid shelters when the sirens sounded again.

The U-Bahn stations were turning more and more into emergency accommodations. People camped out on the platforms—entire families with their luggage; some had set themselves up quite a little home. They had either lost the roof over their heads or else were too afraid to stay there.

At quarter after seven I raced down Waitzstrasse, where the Löwensteins had been living for a while with another family after having been bombed out for the second time.

The three of them were now all living in one large room, where everything looked totally chaotic. What was left of the handmade furniture with the lions' heads from their big house in Stralsund was standing lined up, crowded along the wall. In the middle of the room there were two double beds side by side.

Hans-Oskar wasn't there today. I sat down at the dining table with his parents, and we exchanged news. "Nathan wrote," I said. "Another shipment will be coming soon."

Then Hanna said, "I think we should consider what kind of escape plans Rudolph can arrange for us. Yes, despite the mess-up with Miriam. The man has such good connections! Who knows how much longer all this will go on."

"I think there should be enough money for another large-scale escape operation," her husband added.

"I'll mention it in my next letter," I responded. "Although I don't have good feelings about Rudolph. I know we need him, but we should be careful."

"We also have to take something else into consideration," said Fritz Löwenstein. "Precisely because we don't know how much longer the war will last. Maybe it will be over faster than we think—then what will we do with all the money? Overnight it would lose its value!"

I hadn't thought of that.

"We could buy securities" was Hanna's concise suggestion. "We should ask around cautiously. That would get us through any currency devaluation."

We discussed back and forth for a while. Should we spend the money for a large-scale escape, or should we make a "safe investment"? But was anything safe nowadays? In any case, we definitely still required a ton of money for the day-to-day needs of the people in the underground whom we took care of.

"Are you taking some money with you today?" asked Fritz Löwenstein, as the doorbell rang. Zwi, who was coming to pick me up, used the special ring. The question my "finance minister" posed was a rhetorical one, since it had already been arranged. He handed me ten thousand marks wrapped in newspaper.

Zwi looked good with the blond quiff hanging down on his forehead. He had a dynamic gait and a self-confident smile. I had only seen him for short moments in the previous few days, and I was looking forward to spending the evening with him. He greeted us: "Well, folks, finished already?"

"Do we have anything to eat at home?" I answered the question with a question. He smiled. "In the basement for sure."

We didn't stay much longer. The Löwensteins and I had discussed everything we had to, so Zwi and I headed off toward the Westkreuz S-Bahn station. Back then there was a direct connection from there to the Wedding district. We didn't talk much as we walked; it was less conspicuous that way. And it gave me a moment to review the day in my head.

Once we got home I discussed the coming day with Zwi. We ate dinner, and if luck was with us we could finish our plans—around that time we were taking care of thirty or forty illegals—before the next air raid alarm sounded. There was a major air raid every night; that much was certain.

We had already gotten into bed. "If Rudolph organizes a new escape route," I murmured sleepily and kissed Zwi on his soft lips, "then you'll go to Switzerland on the first round!" With tender hugs we dozed off to sleep. We had long since stopped sleeping in the nude; when the alarm sounded we had to get up and out much too quickly for that.

This time it came around midnight. We hurried into our air raid shelter, dead tired, moving almost automatically. The bombs weren't falling in Wedding tonight. We could hear the planes, hear the explosions in the Tiergarten and Mitte districts, hear the bombers slowly turn and disappear. By two in the morning we were back in bed at the end of an ordinary day.

AXEL RUDOLPH WAS NOT ABLE to find out about any new escape routes for us. Instead, he included us a few times in sabotage acts. They were for the British, but of course he never admitted that to us. In January 1945 he needed four people to serve as lookouts; a bomb was supposed to be in a side building of the IG Farben factory in Lichterfelde. I went with three guys from our group, and we watched the street until it was over. That was the first time I ever saw a building blow up— from below, not from above like in an air raid.

In return, Rudolph got weapons for us. The situation was getting more confusing by the day, and we had resolved that at least the inner circle of our group should not remain defenseless. I distributed five or six of the pistols. I didn't know how to handle the thing, and mine ended up in Frau Peipe's basement, where I had started a small temporary storage, with food, my files and receipts, and also personal notes and poems of mine.

Since the prospects of an escape were becoming more and more improbable, we decided to concentrate on the option of a "safe investment"— even Nathan had agreed with that idea. I told Dreyer about it, and the next time we got together, not even ten days later, he was beaming with delight as he reported, "I have something for you. I know a Jew in the underground named Lustig. He deals in jewelry and other hot merchandise. He makes his living from it."

Paul Dreyer had evidently already gotten pretty involved in the whole thing, because Lustig had gone so far as to give him a bag full of "objects for sale" for us to look at. That would have to be discussed with Fritz Löwenstein. We went to him directly, and Dreyer unpacked his treasures: jewelry, gold, unset gems.

Things clicked quickly for Löwenstein. "What? He gave you all of this just to show us? What kind of collateral did you have to put up?" None at all. That sounded very suspicious. On top of that, they were relatively inexpensive, considering the quality. On the other hand, the end of the war was rapidly approaching, and there were more than enough acts of desperation. . . .

After an extended discussion we decided Dreyer should arrange a meeting between us and Lustig. Not until later did it come to me that even a fence would have known that our money would be of little use so shortly before the end of the war.

We had already wandered into a trap. The man who called himself Lustig was one of Stella's stalking colleagues. For him it promised to be a big catch. Through a German "traitor" he had made contact with a whole group of Jews living illegally—a single individual would never still have had so much money.

Paul Dreyer was arrested in his office on March 1, when he was about to return the "sample" jewelry to Lustig. The snatchers had two Gestapo men with them. Elly Peipe was arrested too. Then the proficient, merciless interrogation and torture machine went into action. They wouldn't have endured it very long.

During these days Zwi and I were often on the go together, all over the city. The final months of the war were unbearable. You could tell with every step that things were going downhill. Nothing worked anymore— but I must say that the Germans kept the everyday infrastructure going remarkably well and remarkably long for a country at war. On that March 2 we didn't get back to the apartment on Utrechter Strasse until late at night, absolutely exhausted.

The building superintendent was standing around in the courtyard as we walked up. He greeted us, staring. For a second that seemed strange to me, since we rarely saw him at all, much less at one in the morning. But he was such a typical Berlin super that his grumbling and gaping seemed to fit perfectly.

"Oh, is it an air raid?" I said. And his response: "No, no, they'll be coming later tonight. Go on and go to bed, there's time to sleep a little." So we went to bed, tired, almost like an old married couple. We were used to each other, loving without thinking about it; nothing very special went on between the sheets.

At 4:00, maybe 4:30, in the morning, they were standing in our room: Rolf Isaaksohn, another Jewish snatcher, and two SS men. They had come in through the bathroom window of the ground-floor apartment, and their weapons were pointing at us. Zwi grabbed for his gun, which was lying next to the bed, but I shouted at him, "Leave it! It's pointless!"

Whoever might have survived a shootout, it certainly wouldn't have been us. Everything proceeded very calmly. We slowly got up. Zwi was desperate; you could see it on his face. He knew from experience what was in store for us. The second Jewish henchman even recognized him. "Aren't you Abrahamssohn?" He had helped arrest Zwi the first time in Karlshorst.

I felt ice-cold inside. When we starting walking down the street, I said quietly to Isaaksohn: "The war is over. You don't have to bring us in anymore, you know that." He shrugged his shoulders. "What else can I do?"

I didn't have to start in with the fate of our Jewish people; the glances we exchanged said it all. Instead I made him a concrete proposal: "I'll kick you in the balls and you simply fall down. Then the case will be closed as far as you're concerned." Of course that never would have worked, but in such a moment you see even the most improbable of ideas as a minuscule chance.

"Forget it," he answered. "Do you really think there's a future for your Zionism?"

"I was thinking about *your* future," I answered dryly. "How are things going to look for you a few months down the road?"

He remained cold. "I'll be long gone." He was wrong; they got him.

By now we had reached the Jewish Hospital on Schulstrasse. Lea Jacob crossed my mind; she was certainly still working there. So now they had caught us after all.

But what had happened to Paul Dreyer and Elly Peipe?

The Gestapo had gotten our address from them. Dreyer was beaten up badly during the interrogation. Within a week he was sentenced to fifteen years in prison for "aiding and abetting Jews" and for "treason."

He tried to improve his situation during the questioning by claiming he didn't know we were Jews. Then why did he help us at all? "Because they were such nice, pretty boys." The poor idiot exposed himself as gay, in hopes that that might help him. Instead it brought him additional battering.

I saw him again a few months after the liberation, at Mamsi's. He looked absolutely terrible and told me what had happened to him in prison. They had set two specially trained dogs on him—specialists in testicles and ears. He lost those body parts entirely; there wasn't the slightest trace of outer ear to be seen, and he was virtually deaf. As concerns the other body part, he said all that was left was a hole for peeing.

It is a mystery to me how he survived it all. He was a well-respected man in his company and lived to a ripe old age, but evidently he had become a bit odd. The last time I saw him was in the late 1970s in Berlin, in Café Kranzler—still an impressive figure. I wrote down everything I wanted to say, and he spoke almost without taking a breath. It was strange. He told me—he was around seventy to my fifty-five—that he had by no

means given up on sex; there was another spot that had a lot of sensa-
tion. . . . I got chills thinking about it.

Elly Peipe had been sent to Ravensbrück, the women's concentration
camp. She survived her imprisonment less traumatically; after the war, she
lived in Hamburg until her death in February 1999. In 1993, one day after
her eightieth birthday, she and other so-called silent helpers received a
standing ovation from the three hundred and fifty guests at a gala dinner
in their honor organized by the Jewish Community in Berlin.

I sat in solitary confinement and was very calm. At first it was like being
in shock. Although I knew of the danger facing Zwi and me, I didn't feel
a thing. Maybe it was even a relief of sorts; ever since my release from
Rosenstrasse two years earlier, I had been living under constant pressure,
doubly threatened by the persecutors and by the "enemy" bombs. Now it
had all been for nothing.

We didn't have a ghost of a chance. When Zwi was arrested the first
time there had been almost no incriminating evidence. Now they had stacks
of files. I had always kept accurate records of expenses, luckily without
names or addresses. They also got hold of personal notes and poems I had
written, which was even more humiliating and painful.

As the inner numbing gradually started to thaw, I grew despairing. I
was horrified by the thought of interrogation and torture. The first thing we
had to do was sign our death sentences. That was part of the treacherous
methods of the Gestapo; the victims had to sign their own death sentences,
thus giving up their resistance and their selves. My thoughts were racing,
but no matter what I thought of in a helpless effort to spark a bit of hope,
it all seemed senseless. In those hours I considered hanging myself.

The men guarding us were not from the SS; they were ordinary policemen. For some reason they all happened to come from Leipzig, in Saxony.
They were generally decent to us, sometimes even friendly. That day one of
them saved me without even realizing what he was doing. He had agreed,
at Zwi's request, to bring me something. It was a folded-up handkerchief
with a lock of Zwi's hair.

Zwi must have sensed how bad I was feeling. What kind of message
could he give me—to say he loved me? He cut off a lock of his hair. I still
have it today. At that moment, it was just what I needed to find some courage to continue.

I had a lot of time to think while I was there. And even then, in the
hands of the worst enemies, I felt neither rage nor hatred. I was infinitely
exhausted and depressed. I despised the Nazis, and it made me feel desperate to realize that that didn't affect them in the least.

Later I often asked myself why I didn't feel more vindictive. Maybe my religious faith played a role in the situation. Only God can take vengeance and punish, not a human being. Feelings of hatred are an expression of powerlessness, and I always concentrated on being as strong as possible, for myself and for others.

I allowed my thoughts to delve to a deeper philosophical level only when there was some chance it would help me. Other than that, I tried my very best to stay out of the way of the dangers and conflicts that threatened me. And I mustered strength from the individual moments of happiness that I was always able to wring out of life, no matter how dire the straits. That was how my survival egoism worked.

ABOUT A WEEK AFTER we were arrested, Walter Dobberke visited me in my cell. He was the director of the camp. Originally a regular police detective, in his thirty-seven years he had already worked his way up to SS Hauptsturmführer, equivalent to a captain. Dobberke was uncanny because he seemed so inconspicuous, so average, so normal. He was of medium height, strong, somewhat boorish, with light, thin hair, no glasses, no beard. At first glance he seemed pretty harmless. Without a uniform he wasn't very remarkable, and even in uniform . . . .

Dobberke was usually pretty friendly and lighthearted with me. His questions were clever, he could laugh, and he rarely became violent. That was the Walter Dobberke of the last two months of the war. The born policeman would only get bitterly angry when he caught someone obviously lying. Then he would strike out, with either his fists or a bullwhip. But he was also capable of respecting his opponent—if it was someone he found interesting and took seriously. He never touched me.

That day, he stood before me, scrutinizing me a long time and then finally saying, "So, you really did work your butt off, didn't you?"

I looked at him blankly, as though I didn't know what he was talking about. It could win me some time, and sometimes it made people hesitate a little, since they thought they hadn't expressed themselves clearly.

"Yeah, the traitor! You've got to thank the traitor!" Now I really didn't understand a word he was saying. "That Thomas Mann who's with the enemy and is always poisoning people's minds over the radio waves! Yesterday he said, 'Günther Kaplan and his friends were liberated by the Red Army in Landsberg on the Oder.' He's a liar and a traitor!"

Now, that's a very nebulous story. Until today there is no documentation that Thomas Mann ever said anything like that. In his radio reports from the war years, which were later published, there is nothing of the sort. The whole style of the talks was very different. But sometimes Mann evidently added little bits of information, such as news briefs, which he didn't receive until he was already in the studio. Maybe it was something like that? The BBC never archived the tapes with Thomas Mann's talks, so the manuscripts are the only documentation, and they didn't include such "news" inserts.

On the other hand, I didn't know anyone in Landsberg on the Oder. Once he heard that I had been arrested, Nathan Schwalb had moved heaven and earth trying to find out where I was. His couriers were supposed to spread the news about me as far and as officially as possible, in hopes of somehow helping me. Possibly that's how the story made its way to the BBC in London. Could "Landsberg" have been a code word or a bluff?

I suspect the latter, if these words really did ever make it on the air at all. The fact that Dobberke came to me could be interpreted as a sign of "respect." My seeming prominence didn't make me a preferred target for attacks, questioning, and harassment, as it might have six months earlier. The war was in its final hours, and everyone was starting to think about saving their own skin. Whatever the real reason, I was given suede gloves whenever I was handcuffed, and they generally treated me decently.

Or was it all very different? Had Dobberke invented such a complicated story to sound me out to see if I would talk? Did he want to make me feel safe and soften me up with the gloves? By making it seem like he already knew everything, did he want to lure me into giving up?

I didn't get it. But I was certain that my only chance was to exaggerate my activities as much as I could and make them seem as important as possible. I had nothing to lose and everything to gain.

Two days later Zwi and I were brought to the Gestapo on Französische Strasse to be interrogated. Two marshals transported us in handcuffs by U-Bahn. The other passengers just stared.

Zwi and I were even allowed to talk to each other. Of course we couldn't make any giant plans. We tried to encourage each other, putting all our feelings into the few gazes we had time for.

Zwi was brought to a medium-ranking officer, and I was suddenly standing opposite Erich Möller, the notorious Gestapo murderer. He had the grumpy, dull face of a terrier, with empty, evil eyes and hanging cheeks. He was a stocky bastard, lurking behind his desk, and I almost died from the shock.

Because we knew each other! Fifteen years earlier, he was the owner of a tobacco kiosk on the outskirts of Berlin, and Margot and I had delivered cigarettes to him . . . and as a tip we would always get a lollipop. . . . Now here we were face to face.

Everyone knew that Möller was the type that used thumbscrews. And on his desk was precisely that—thumbscrews. He put my briefcase next to them. Möller showed no emotion.

"So, whaddya been thinking the whole time?" He sounded like a school principal. He picked up my elegant Swiss pigskin briefcase. "And this wasn't made by us, either," he declared.

I didn't utter a word. What could I respond to sentences like that anyway? Möller fixed his dull stare on the briefcase before opening it. The first thing he pulled out was a piece of stationery from Axel Rudolph; the letterhead had his alias, Count Kronenburg. "So, who is this Count Kronenburg?"

I started talking casually. "That's a man we've known for quite some time. He's not Jewish, no way. . . ."

"What business do you have with him?" he interrupted.

"I don't know exactly," I was thinking as I went along, "and I don't want to start any rumors, but"—and here I paused for effect, smiling at him mischievously—"I think he and my sister had a bit of a friendship."

Of course that didn't interest Möller in the least. "I don't want to hear such bullshit!" He knew Kronenburg was an agent, and my diversionary tactics didn't impress him. He just shook his head back and forth, dissatisfied, then turned back to the briefcase. I was on tenterhooks. All he had to do was pull out one single invoice and I wouldn't have had any choice but to lay it on really thick about the whole Swiss connection. But that wouldn't have been easy for me.

Instead he grabbed one of my poems! "But you had time to write some gay-boy love poems, huh?"

He held the piece of paper up in front of me. I stared at my handwriting, unbelieving and taken by surprise. At first I thought it was one of the two poems I had written for Zwi. Wrong. But how did Möller know about us? They must have gotten that out of Dreyer. No, this poem had actually been written for Karla Wagenberg; I had written it a year earlier.

I See Your Picture

I see your picture,
    and behind the thin glass
    your life appears to me
    like reality.
As though you were by me
    and your hand held me
    so motherly and soft
    as things once were.
Your eye looks at me
    with cheerful confidence.

> And smiling, your mouth
> brings words of love to me.
> Staggering I reach for you—
>   but you are so far away, so far.
>   You were my offering
>   to the old times.
> You cannot hear me?
>   My cursing and my screams
>   never make it through to you,
>   it is in vain.
> Through your sacrifice,
>   the flame blazes up,
>   that which joins us and strengthens
>   us in struggle!
> Fight against your murderers!
>   Fight every war and blaze
>   committed by human hands
>   and whose victim is you.
> I see your picture,
>   and I look firmly into your eyes,
>   as a vow.
> The thin glass shattered.

I had written that in a very emotional moment that seemed lightyears away. In that moment of weakness, Möller could have gotten me. But he was too dumb. And he didn't understand the poem anyway.

The door to his office was open, intentionally. I could hear Zwi getting beaten and screaming in the next room. These bastards! I clenched my teeth and was fully alert again.

Möller imitated a dissatisfied diva. "You do still have to tell me a little something, you hear me? It's been a bit skimpy so far!"

"But I wrote you a protocol, like Herr Dobberke demanded—thirty handwritten pages!" I protested. "It contains everything I have to say."

Unfortunately he hadn't seen it. Maybe it was better that way, because my "confession" was nothing but a fine display of chutzpah. In it, I had "talked." I named names. Most of them were high-ranking diplomats from countries allied with Germany who had long since left Berlin. I described such a network of partisans and agents and helpers that it was a real joy to write, and the whole thing was one big pack of lies.

I had no idea what the Gestapo had found out by that time. Later I heard that the extent of my conspiratorial activities, the way I outlined them, had made quite an impression. Even if none of it was true.

And now Möller hadn't even seen the protocol. I didn't want to tell him what was in it, because I was afraid I would contradict myself, but I did have another trick up my sleeve. "You're no big hero," he announced with an almost paternal mutter, still preoccupied with the poem, as he looked at my small, wiry stature.

This is my chance, I thought, and I drew a deep breath, "We've met before, Herr Sturmbannführer." He looked disbelieving, reluctant. "Yes, yes. At the tobacco kiosk that you and your wife had in Ahrensfelde." His expression lightened briefly. Did he remember? "You always gave me and my sister lollipops, two for a pfennig."

He jostled in his seat. "That's enough now!" he grunted. "You can go."

I was told to wait outside. The man who was giving Zwi a going-over wasn't finished yet. Then he came toward me in the hall, evidently after having spoken with Möller.

"So, you were hot for some jewelry? Did you put on some pearls and wiggle your little behinds, huh? Did you fuck each other in the ass?"

I stayed calm. "Ask Abrahamssohn what we did. He doesn't even know the word."

And the man really did go back in to ask Zwi. The door was still ajar, and I could hear Zwi answer, surprised but truthfully, "No, we didn't do that. I don't even know what that is."

There were no words for the affections we shared that these brutes would have understood. The man could see that Zwi's surprise was genuine, and he left him alone. They couldn't pin us down so easily as gay.

The marshal who had brought us there couldn't believe his eyes. "It's a miracle that you got out of there like that. No one comes out of there like that," he said to me. We rode back on the U-Bahn, even though Zwi was bloody and swollen. Again, all the other passengers stared—and said not a word. Just don't get involved. In March 1945 they had other problems.

We went back to our cells. Möller didn't call for us again.

Days passed. Every now and then Dobberke would question us. Zwi didn't talk. I further developed my far-reaching connections to "international Jewry" and didn't give away anything about things closer, that is, Berlin.

The bombardments were coming more and more often. Everyone in the Jewish Hospital would have to go down to the basement rooms and corridors, regardless of whether they were doctors or patients, Gestapo or prisoners. That somehow gave me a great feeling of satisfaction, to know that even Dobberke had to crawl away and hide. "Aren't you afraid?" he snapped at me once while standing in the hallway in front of my barred door.

"Of course I am," I answered. "I'm just as afraid of the bombs as you are."

My mother visited us as often as she could and would bring us something to eat. She herself had recently been in St. Hedwig's Hospital for an operation on her foot. There were hardly any trains or streetcars running anymore, and this woman dragged herself from Alexanderplatz all the way to the Wedding district to bring her son food parcels in jail.

The third time she came she had gotten a little pullcart, since she couldn't walk anymore, and Heinz Blümel pulled her. That must have been a sight that fit right in with the atmosphere of catastrophe of the last few weeks. An almost-fifty-year-old in a little wagon getting pulled by a hunchback through the ruins. . . . That day she said to me, "Son, I can't manage to visit you anymore. At least not right now. Please don't be angry."

Instead she sent Aunt Martha. Until the very end they stood by me and tried to help where they could—to help *me*, the dangerous head of a Zionist resistance group! And their risk was not small, whether they were Christians or not.

The food was of course cut open and checked, but I got it; even the ham was still on the bread! The wardens were decent in that respect.

When I was taken upstairs for questioning, we went along a corridor lined with books from the hospital library. Once when I was returning to my cell I asked a police officer if I could take a book to read. He nodded, and I discovered a book that seemed almost surreal in this context, *Zeitgenossen über Theodor Herzl* (Contemporaries on Theodor Herzl). There I was sitting in a Gestapo prison cell, with bombs falling all around me, and I could intoxicate myself with the fascinating portrait of this great Zionist in articles and recollections by fascinated contemporaries. Some of the authors were even crowned heads, both Germans and foreigners.

But not all the wardens were friendly. I had once just said goodbye to Aunt Martha when one of them started giving her a hard time, apparently assuming she was my mother. "So you still haven't had enough of the Jews? Why didn't you get divorced in time?"

Martha gave him a dressing-down equal to that of the most obstinate of Nazis. "You are mistaken! This is my nephew, and I am the wife of the engineer Ludwig who builds bridges for our Wehrmacht so they can push on to victory!" That shut him up. The troops were long since in retreat.

A few days later the door suddenly opened and Kurt Wallach was thrown into my cell.

You often read about it in books, but it's difficult to imagine what a torture victim looks like. Since that day I know. They had literally smashed him to pieces.

Every part of his body was swollen, his too-tight clothes all torn; he couldn't have even taken them off anymore. Strangely enough, he still had his teeth. But he couldn't even lie down on his own, he was so covered with bruises and cuts. I leaned against the wall, and he slid down along me onto the mattress.

It was clear that they would continue to interrogate him. I tried to prepare him by telling him what he could say without disclosing anything. I struggled to think of harmless things to drill into him, but there was no sense. He said virtually nothing anymore, merely nodded and mumbled to himself.

He wasn't even able to tell me what had happened. The others told me later.

IN EARLY 1945 I HAD FOUND LODGINGS for Kurt together with Stefan Wechsler, who had escaped from Buchenwald concentration camp, in an abandoned apartment in Friedrichshain. After Zwi and I were arrested, the rest of the group of course tried to somehow continue the work.

So one day they had given Mousey the job of picking up horsemeat from Tutti and Bruno, a couple who had a restaurant, and distributing it to various illegals. He was given the corresponding list with the recipients' names. That evening the Allies flew a fierce air raid. The Mitte and Friedrichshain districts were in flames.

In all the excitement, Stefan and Kurt broke one of the fundamental rules of living underground. One of them used the bathroom in the apartment and then flushed the toilet! It was an unmistakable sign that someone was still in a building that was supposedly empty.

The air raid warden called the police. All doors were kept open in case of fire, so it didn't take them long to find the only locked apartment and break down the door. Stefan started shooting—with one of our pistols—wounding two policemen and the warden. Then the two of them took off. But Kurt lost his breath, and they nabbed him within about a hundred yards.

Stefan got away but was wounded. He made it to Frau Szimke's, where he ran into Fräulein Schmidt. He told her about Kurt's arrest and, more important, that Kurt still had the address list with him!

I have often thought how indescribably foolish that was. I would never have let Kurt have such a list. When I was in charge, there never even was a list; I always had all the names and addresses in my head. But of course, no one was really in charge anymore.

In a frantic hurry, Stefan and Fräulein Schmidt sat down and tried to reconstruct the list. By now "Schmitty" had a pretty good overview of who was living where. There were thirteen addresses on the list. That meant the lives of about thirty-six illegals were in danger—without their knowing it—not to mention Stefan and Schmidt themselves, Szimke, Amnon and Mordechai Wallach, and God knows who else's names the Gestapo might've been able to beat out of Kurt.

That same night of the heavy bombing, Fräulein Schmidt was absolutely fearless, hopping onto her bicycle and pedaling throughout all of northeastern Berlin to alert the people. And she made it. All of those in hiding were warned in time, and not a single person was caught.

Someone who was not in hiding, however, was Zwi's Aunt Marie in Blankenburg, and she was supposed to get some of the horsemeat too. She received the Gestapo with a clear head. "Where is your husband?" "He's at work, where else?" "Do you know what he is involved in? Getting food on the black market!"

Now, Aunt Marie was a clever woman, and she had no intention of making things more complicated than necessary. "I have a food rations card, why should I get food on the black market? Where did you get that idea from?"

She denied everything, and the Gestapo believed her. She looked far too harmless with her thick glasses. And besides, the snatchers had not had any success in finding any of the other people on the list; they must have started wondering about its validity at all.

There was only one person Fräulein Schmidt had not been able to warn, since she hadn't been at home, and that was Ruth Gomma. Everyone was terribly worried about Mamsi and her mother. It turned out to be a really close call, as Mamsi told me after it was all over.

The next morning, Rolf Isaaksohn and an SS man appeared at her apartment on Binzstrasse. Mamsi and her mother had since moved in with a Christian friend, one floor down. Fräulein Schmidt hadn't even known that.

The friend was at work and Mamsi's mother was shopping when Mamsi heard banging on the door a flight above her. She took heart, stepped into the stairwell, and shouted up, "Who are you looking for?" She was a well-groomed housewife with glasses and an apron. She looked like your typical nosy neighbor. "We're looking for the tenant of this apartment, the Jewess Künstler!"

That had been Mamsi's last name ever since she had married a Herr Künstler, from whom she was, by the way, already divorced. Since Mamsi's name was on the list, the Gestapo men considered her a criminal, and that was justification enough for them to call her a "Jewess."

"Oh, her," Mamsi must have really gulped, "she and her mother are at relatives in the Spreewald forest area. Been there for weeks already. Do you want to come in and have a cup of coffee?"

The two men weren't at all suspicious and accepted her offer. Mamsi, of course, was shitting bricks. Her mother could come home any minute, and since she was hard of hearing she would certainly say something wrong before Mamsi could make it clear to her just who her coffee guests were. What should she do?

Mamsi straightened up some things in the apartment like an industrious housewife and managed to stay near the window. And there she saw her mother shuffling along the street with her groceries. Mamsi kept making signals to her mother, terrified that her "guests" would notice and her mother wouldn't. But it worked. The mother never came up the stairs, and after they finished drinking the watery coffee, the two men took their leave. "Let us know as soon as Künstler comes back!" Mamsi promised she would.

Fräulein Schmidt's fast action saved thirty-six people's lives.

It was not until after the war that I heard "our" prostitute's whole story. Her private apartment was in the building where Alfred Lindau's cardboard packaging factory was located, on Georgenkirchstrasse. Even back then the ordinary workers would make jokes about her. Finally I realized why she never offered to let people stay in her own apartment. It wasn't for security reasons but because she already had someone hiding there—none other than the man we once shared an apartment with, Erich Nehlhans!

When in early 1944 he didn't know where to go anymore, since the Romanians he was living with were also in danger, he went to see his old acquaintance Alfred Lindau. There was no longer much business for the factory; small carton factories were hardly doing any work for the war effort anymore. So Lindau decided to make a cardboard hiding place in the storage basement for Nehlhans. He must have mentioned it to Fräulein Schmidt at some point, because she took charge of taking care of him until the end of the war.

I didn't see Erich Nehlhans again until 1946 at a Zionist conference in Zurich. There he told me the story of how he survived. "My wife took care of me the entire time," he said.

"But Edith was murdered," I said, confused.

"No, I have a new wife, Gad," he said and looked a bit impish. It was our Schmitty!

Even back then the two of them had started a relationship, and Fräulein Schmidt remained Erich Nehlhans's partner even after he became the first chairman of the Berlin Jewish Community after the war. Our first—unofficial—First Lady was a former aristocratic Alexanderplatz prostitute!

In 1990 she died at a ripe old age in a senior citizens' home in the Pankow district. She was a quiet, pious gentlewoman with an eventful past that almost no one knew about.

While Zwi and I were in prison, something else also went wrong. The world we had been part of seemed to be falling apart at the seams; everything was collapsing.

Rudi Bernstein took over the correspondence with Switzerland. He sent a postcard to Jizchak Schwersenz—the last from our Berlin group—that enraged Nathan Schwalb:

My dear!   22 March 1945

No good news for you today. Very worried about your children and dear Chuggi, who had an accident. Unfortunately dear Gad and Uncle Heini [Zwi] too. I haven't heard from you in ages; nor from Uncle Schwalby [Nathan]. If at least Kaspi [money] would visit me, I wouldn't worry so much about the other dears who are still here. Please see that your friend, who is here so often on business, comes to visit and brings me news and K [money]. I hope that you do everything you possibly can. Now I'll close, dear Uncle Joachim, with wishes that you really do try to reach me. Your faithful nephew, Rudi.

In one breath, Zwi and I were declared dead and more money was requested for no reason. Nathan was anything but amused.

Apropos "Kaspi," another daring story took place while I was in jail. Fritz Löwenstein was carrying a large sum of money. There wasn't really a need for that, since food procurement always involved smaller amounts, but anyway, he and his son Hans-Oskar were in a restaurant when a group of SS men suddenly stormed in and started a raid.

In his panic, Fritz raced to the men's room and started stuffing the money down the toilet so it wouldn't be found on him. He couldn't flush as fast as he tried to get rid of the stuff. When he returned to his son at the table and they were about to breathe a sigh of relief, Hans-Oskar noticed that he had a picture of Miriam in his breast pocket. Why did the boy have to carry, of all things, a picture of my sister near his heart? He barely managed to sneak out of the room and run up the stairs to the toilets. He got quite a shock—there were still bills floating in the toilet! He pushed and struggled and flushed money and photo scraps down, while the footsteps of the SS were already approaching. At least the problem with the devaluation of the money had been solved. A large portion of the surplus money we had was gone! The Löwenstein father and son were nevertheless arrested and brought to the assembly camp on Schulstrasse.

W E WERE SITTING IN OUR CELL, Mousey and me. It was April. The war was not over yet. Through a little window in our cellar, which was not totally underground, we could see into the courtyard of the parklike hospital grounds. The view was eerily idyllic: lawns, trees, and ivy-covered walls. One day I observed a group of prisoners during their yard exercise—and I discovered my sister, Miriam, and a short time later Hans-Oskar and his father! What a shock! What had happened? How had they been arrested? Earlier that would have meant our deportation, but now? The transports had always been to the east. But now the Russians were to the east and transports had virtually ceased. The last train to Auschwitz had departed on January 5, 1945, as I later found out, and in March the last transports to Sachsenhausen, Ravensbrück, and Theresienstadt took place. Would they shoot us? Or had we meanwhile become important enough to them for the time "afterwards"?

When another package from Aunt Martha arrived, Kurt and I were squatting at opposite walls of the cell. We probably kept our distance because we stank so terribly; otherwise I would have preferred to sit close to him. I unpacked it, and we slowly, silently, ate our way through the contents of the package. In that moment a bomb fell and hit the pavilion directly above us.

But it didn't explode! Or else we would have been blown to smithereens. Only the building extension collapsed. Mousey, who had been sitting on the window side, crawled out and screamed indescribably. The rest of the cellar room was buried. I was lying somewhere under the rubble, alive. The ceiling of our cell was half caved in, the walls too; some earth even made its way in. I couldn't see my hand in front of my face, but I realized that there was a tiny space around me that was still holding. The air was filled with dust, and I had to cough terribly. At first I didn't dare make a sign by knocking, for fear the whole thing would cave in on top of me.

Outside Dobberke was on the scene immediately to check out the situation. Kurt was taken to the hospital ward. And Dobberke gave orders to dig me out: "Whoever gets him out alive can leave the camp with their family." As the last remaining central assembly camp of the Gestapo in Berlin, the hospital housed hundreds of prisoners.

The volunteer was a Hungarian Jew who had been raised in France. I later found out his name was Alexander Timar, and he now lives in New York. He wasn't in the camp with any family members, but he hoped to be able to take a few friends with him to freedom. He started digging. After a little while I noticed what was happening. Water was running into my air space; a pipe had obviously broken somewhere. I started panicking and screamed as loudly as I could, "Water! Water!" They heard me outside, as the top layers of rubble had already been removed, and turned off the water; otherwise I would have drowned.

I could hear the man digging, hitting the rubble with a pick, and screamed again, "To the left! To the left!" so he wouldn't hit me. Then the pressure increased all of a sudden, and I couldn't hear anything anymore.

The pavilion had totally collapsed, and the remains all fell onto my cell.

My liberator had jumped back just in time. He immediately started digging again as soon as the dust had cleared. After a while, the sounds started getting closer again. I began screaming; he answered—in French of course. So I started directing my rescue with "*À droite!*" and "*À gauche!*" and "*Attention!*" Then something crumbled above me, a crack appeared, and I finally saw some light. I could see people, including my sister, who shouted, "We're almost there; you'll be out in a minute!"

They dragged me partway out. That is, my head and shoulders were sticking out but the rest of my body was still caught fast. I got hysterical. The sky darkened, and the next bombers could already be heard. I was so afraid I didn't know what I was screaming anymore. "Pull me out, I don't care if my leg comes off! Just pull!" I didn't feel anything anymore, no pain, just shock and panic. It took quite a while till they finally got me all the way out. The only thing that was still under the rubble was one of my wonderful Swiss shoes.

Other than that I was all there. Numerous broken bones and bruises and scrapes and cuts, but my arms and legs were all still attached. They carried me to the top floor of the main building, into a big hospital room. It was there that I finally lost consciousness.

When I came to, Lea Jacob was bending over me. I was relieved to see a familiar face. There were eight beds in my room. The other inhabitants all had privileged status, and Lea warned me not to talk too openly with them. No one was all too sure which side they were on.

The doctor explained to me that he wanted to do only what was absolutely necessary, so they wouldn't put me back in the cellar. "It's a struggle against time," he said. I had a fever almost all the time, which was the main reason for keeping me in the hospital ward. There was always an SS man at the door to my room. You have to imagine—in the final weeks of the war they had an SS man to spare to guard me! I was certain of one thing: Either I would make it half alive until we were liberated, or I would die up there in the hospital bed. I would not return to that hole.

The personnel evidently had precise instructions as to what to do when there was an air raid. Other patients were taken to the basement, but I wasn't. My bed was pushed into the stairwell. That was despicable. If we were hit, the shrapnel would have made mincemeat out of me.

On April 20 the situation came to a head. Lea Jacob came to me and whispered what had happened. Möller had contacted Dobberke and ordered the immediate "liquidation" of the assembly camp. A Jewish boy who had been polishing the camp director's shoes at the time had overheard enough of the conversation, and the news spread like wildfire among the prisoners. They had decided to talk to Dobberke and demand that he release all of them!

The next day I was carried back downstairs on a stretcher. This time I ended up in a larger room. As I looked around the basement I saw, in a corner half in shadows, my Zwi. He was as pale as death. I was happy and startled at the same time.

"How are you doing?" I asked.

"Gad, they let all the others out today; even Miriam was released. Everyone had to sign a paper saying that Dobberke refused to liquidate the camp. They gave me back my things. And now they bring you here too. What's it supposed to mean? Why don't they let us out? It's a trick; they must want to shoot us."

He was absolutely shattered. There was nothing I could say to him. I could hardly even move. There was nothing to do but wait and see.

The bombardments were unceasing. The hospital shook down to the foundations. But we didn't hear any more voices in the building.

In the evening, footsteps approached our cell. There he was standing in front of us, Walter Dobberke, the boss. He pulled out two letters and tore them up. The death sentences we had signed.

Was he planning to finish us off unofficially, right then and there? No, he was acting friendly. He had something else with him—our release certificates, dated April 21, 1945.

Without a word he handed them to us and then said, almost in passing, "I need a place to go for a few days. You certainly have quarters where I could be undisturbed. Where are they?"

Did he want to make a deal with us? I thought quickly. We just had to make it through the next few days. I decided to wager high stakes. "Yes, at Schulz's on Schönhauser Allee!"

That was where our old friend Werner Schulz, the baker's son, was now living. Shortly before we had been arrested, I had arranged for a few people to stay there, and the rest of the weapons from Rudolph were stored there too. If Dobberke really had gone to Schulz's apartment—which I didn't really believe he would do—there would have been a wild shootout.

But someone who definitely was not carrying a weapon anymore was Dobberke—I could see that as he turned to go. I never did understand what he really wanted from us; in any case, he never showed up on Schönhauser Allee. For him, the war was over.

Dobberke walked out of our cell and left the door open.

The next day was the final battle of Berlin—building by building, street by street. Together with Dobberke, all the Gestapo officials left the hospital. But we didn't know that for sure. We didn't know anything for sure. All we could hear were bombs, machine guns, grenade throwers. The din of the raging battle came closer and closer. The shooting was unremitting, as was the shouting—in Russian. Zwi and I had only one thought: We're in for it now. If the Russians ran into young men, they'd start shooting without asking too many questions! We stayed put.

On April 24 we heard them up above on the hospital grounds. They were from the Red Army—and the Red Cross. A short time later we saw our first Russian soldier. He came into our cellar room. It would have been pointless to run away—and I couldn't run anywhere anyway. He didn't look especially fit for action himself; he was ragged, shot up, wasted.

What would he do with us? What was going on upstairs? Zwi and he and I stared at each other, exchanging silent glances.

The man reached into his pocket. He was here for a reason. He pulled something out—not a weapon, but a piece of paper. Had he read it out upstairs too? He started speaking, to our great surprise in Yiddish! "*Iz do eyner vos heyst Gad Beck?*" Is there someone here named Gad Beck?

That might sound like an incredible coincidence. But it wasn't. Nathan Schwalb had put it out across all his channels that Gad Beck must be somewhere in Berlin in a Gestapo prison. The Soviet troops had gotten the information from the Red Cross. So they were looking specifically for me. There were enough Russian Jews, even if they did not draw much attention to themselves. And this one had found me, in the basement of the Jewish Hospital: "*Iz do eyner vos heyst Gad Beck?*"

I raised my hand wearily. He looked at us and announced solemnly, "*Brider, ir zayt fray!*" Brothers, you are free!

Epilogue

BUT WERE THEY REALLY FREE?
For Gad Beck and Zwi Abrahamssohn, the war was over, but freedom had yet to come. It would take days and months before Germany could even begin to make a new start. And this is where part two of Gad Beck's memoirs set off.

The Soviets made the twenty-two-year-old the first "representative for Jewish affairs" in Berlin—but he soon felt doubt as to how well disposed they really were toward the surviving Jews. With a small group of friends he trudged his way on an adventuresome trek clear across the ruins of Germany to Munich, the "free West." There he received the task from the Hechalutz to gather people from the displaced persons camps and organize their—still illegal—immigration to Palestine. In the course of his efforts, Gad Beck finally met David Ben-Gurion and worked together with him.

In 1947 he too stepped aboard a ship to Eretz Israel, the British secret service on his heels. . . . He was soon followed by Miriam and his parents— and Zwi. And many other friends who survived the war and persecution by the Nazis. After the State of Israel was founded in 1948 and after the first war with the Arabs, a fifteen-year period of settled existence finally began for Gad Beck, a time during which he enjoyed a carefree, "normal," well, almost bourgeois, lifestyle, together with Zwi, in the circle of his family and friends. Though it was by no means boring.

Gad decided not to go into a life of politics. David Ben-Gurion had advised against it: "You don't have the elbows for it!" Instead, he studied psychology and worked in Tel Aviv for Malben, an institution aiding the social integration of the constant influx of immigrants from the diaspora.

In the 1960s Gad Beck was on the road again, especially in Germany. He helped develop the German-Israeli Student Association (BDIS) and gave numerous lectures and seminars. When the children of the Nazi generation in Germany started asking questions of their parents, he contributed with his seminars to help them understand both the answers and the non-answers, as a contemporary, a living witness, who has the ability to bring home history that often seems incomprehensible. His goal has always been to remember and, most important, to share his experience.

During these years, Gad Beck remained just as true to himself and his love of life as before. His active love life spurred him on in the common cause. . . . They call it "bringing people together," don't they?

In 1974 he was called upon by the Jewish Community in Vienna to take charge of the youth work, which had been at a standstill since the war. It was a time of political and intellectual discourse—and the site of a significant encounter. In 1976 Gad met Julius Laufer, who has remained his lifelong companion.

Ever since 1978 Gad Beck has been back living in Berlin. He worked together with Heinz Galinski, head of the Berlin Jewish Community, until Galinski's death in 1992. Together with David Ben-Gurion and Martin Buber, Galinski is the third of Beck's prime role models. Gad Beck spent ten years as director of the Jewish Adult Education Center in Berlin. Today, over seventy years old, he is still in demand, both in Germany and abroad, as a person to talk to when the subject is Jewish life in Germany, today and in the past.

After the exciting story of his youth, in part two of his memoirs "little Gad" will recount just as zestfully the story of the next fifty years of his life.

Published originally under the title:
Und Gad ging zu David
Die Erinnerungen des Gad Beck
herausgegeben von Frank Heibert
© 1995 zebra literaturverlag, Berlin